The Dynasts by Thomas Hardy

AN EPIC-DRAMA OF THE WAR WITH NAPOLEON, IN THREE PARTS

PART THIRD

The Time covered by the Action being about ten Years

"And I heard sounds of insult, shame, and wrong,
And trumpets blown for wars."

Many giants of Literature originate from the shores of these emerald isles; Shakespeare, Dickens, Chaucer, The Brontes and Austen to which most people would willingly add the name Thomas Hardy.

'Far From The Madding Crowd',' Tess Of The D'Urbervilles', 'The Mayor Of Casterbridge' are but three of his literary masterpieces.

In fact, Hardy himself thought he was a poet who wrote novels purely for the money. Indeed his poems were not published until he was in his fifties after his major novels were published and his reputation set. His novels of course continue to influence and mentor our thoughts.

Each is a journey through a mind that creates characters, landscapes and narratives that reveal themselves in rich and textured detail as few other writers are able to do.

Index of Contents

THOMAS HARDY – A CONCISE BIBLIOGRAPHY

I. PHANTOM INTELLIGENCES
THE ANCIENT SPIRIT OF THE YEARS/CHORUS OF THE YEARS.
THE SPIRIT OF THE PITIES/CHORUS OF THE PITIES.
SPIRITS SINISTER AND IRONIC/CHORUSES OF SINISTER AND IRONIC SPIRITS.
THE SPIRIT OF RUMOUR/CHORUS OF RUMOURS.
THE SHADE OF THE EARTH.
SPIRIT MESSENGERS.
RECORDING ANGELS.
II. PERSONS
MEN [The names in lower case are mute figures.]
THE PRINCE REGENT.
The Royal Dukes.
THE DUKE OF RICHMOND.
The Duke of Beaufort.
CASTLEREAGH, Prime Minister.
Palmerston, War Secretary.
PONSONBY, of the Opposition.
BURDETT, of the Opposition.
WHITBREAD, of the Opposition.
Tierney, Romilly, of the Opposition
Other Members of Parliament.
TWO ATTACHES.
A DIPLOMATIST.
Ambassadors, Ministers, Peers, and other persons of Quality
and Office.
....
WELLINGTON.
UXBRIDGE.
PICTON.
HILL.
CLINTON.
Colville.
COLE.
BERESFORD.
Pack and Kempt.
Byng.
Vivian.
W. Ponsonby, Vandeleur, Colquhoun-Grant, Maitland, Adam, and
C. Halkett.
Graham, Le Marchant, Pakenham, and Sir Stapleton Cotton.
SIR W. DE LANCEY.

FITZROY SOMERSET.
COLONELS FRASER, H. HALKETT, COLBORNE, Cameron, Hepburn, LORD
SALTOUN, C. Campbell.
SIR NEIL CAMPBELL.
Sir Alexander Gordon, BRIGDEMAN, TYLER, and other AIDES.
CAPTAIN MERCER.
Other Generals, Colonels, and Military Officers.
Couriers.

A SERGEANT OF DRAGOONS.
Another SERGEANT.
A SERGEANT of the 15th HUSSARS.
A SENTINEL. Batmen.
AN OFFICER'S SERVANT.
Other non-Commissioned Officers and Privates of the British Army.
English Forces.
....
SIR W. GELL, Chamberlain to the Princess of Wales.
MR. LEGH, a Wessex Gentleman.
Another GENTLEMAN.
THE VICAR OF DURNOVER.
Signor Tramezzini and other members of the Opera Company.
M. Rozier, a dancer.

LONDON CITIZENS.
A RUSTIC and a YEOMAN.
A MAIL-GUARD.
TOWNSPEOPLE, Musicians, Villagers, etc.
....
THE DUKE OF BRUNSWICK.
THE PRINCE OF ORANGE.
Count Alten.
Von Ompteda, Baring, Duplat, and other Officers of the King's-
German Legion.
Perponcher, Best, Kielmansegge, Wincke, and other Hanoverian
Officers.
Bylandt and other Officers of the Dutch-Belgian troops.
SOME HUSSARS.
King's-German, Hanoverian, Brunswick, and Dutch-Belgian Forces.
....
BARON VAN CAPELLEN, Belgian Secretary of State.
The Dukes of Arenberg and d'Ursel.
THE MAYOR OF BRUSSELS.
CITIZENS AND IDLERS of Brussels.
....
NAPOLEON BONAPARTE.
JOSEPH BONAPARTE.
Jerome Bonaparte.

THE KING OF ROME.
Eugene de Beauharnais.
Cambaceres, Arch-Chancellor to Napoleon.
TALLEYRAND.
CAULAINCOURT.
DE BAUSSET.
....
MURAT, King of Naples.
SOULT, Napoleon's Chief of Staff.
NEY.
DAVOUT.
MARMONT.
BERTHIER.
BERTRAND.
BESSIERES.
AUGEREAU, MACDONALD, LAURISTON, CAMBRONNE.
Oudinot, Friant, Reille, d'Erlon, Drouot, Victor, Poniatowski,
Jourdan, and other Marshals, and General and Regimental
Officers of Napoleon's Army.
RAPP, MORTIER, LARIBOISIERE.
Kellermann and Milhaud.
COLONELS FABVRIER, MARBOT, MALLET, HEYMES, and others.
French AIDES and COURIERS.
DE CANISY, Equerry to the King of Rome.
COMMANDANT LESSARD.
Another COMMANDANT.
BUSSY, an Orderly Officer.
SOLDIERS of the Imperial Guard and others.
STRAGGLERS; A MAD SOLDIER.
French Forces.
....
HOUREAU, BOURDOIS, and Ivan, physicians.
MENEVAL, Private Secretary to Napoleon.
DE MONTROND, an emissary of Napoleon's.
Other Secretaries to Napoleon.
CONSTANT, Napoleon's Valet.
ROUSTAN, Napoleon's Mameluke.
TWO POSTILLIONS.
A TRAVELLER.
CHAMBERLAINS and Attendants.
SERVANTS at the Tuileries.
FRENCH CITIZENS and Townspeople.
....
THE KING OF PRUSSIA.
BLUCHER.
MUFFLING, Wellington's Prussian Attache.
GNEISENAU.
Zieten.

Bulow.
Kleist, Steinmetz, Thielemann, Falkenhausen.
Other Prussian General and Regimental Officers.
A PRUSSIAN PRISONER of the French.
Prussian Forces.
....
FRANCIS, Emperor of Austria.
METTERNICH, Chancellor and Foreign Minister.
Hardenberg.
NEIPPERG
Schwarzenberg, Kleinau, Hesse-Homburg, and other Austrian Generals.
Viennese Personages of rank and fashion.
Austrian Forces.
....
THE EMPEROR ALEXANDER of Russia.
Nesselrode.
KUTUZOF.
Bennigsen.
Barclay de Tolly, Dokhtorof, Bagration, Platoff, Tchichagoff,
Miloradovitch, and other Russian Generals.
Rostopchin, Governor of Moscow.
SCHUVALOFF, a Commissioner.
A RUSSIAN OFFICER under Kutuzof.
Russian Forces.
Moscow Citizens.
....
Alava, Wellington's Spanish Attache.
Spanish and Portuguese Officers.
Spanish and Portuguese Forces.
Spanish Citizens.
....
Minor Sovereigns and Princes of Europe.
LEIPZIG CITIZENS.

WOMEN
CAROLINE, PRINCESS OF WALES.
The Duchess of York.
THE DUCHESS OF RICHMOND.
The Duchess of Beaufort.
LADY H. DARYMPLE
Lady de Lancey.
LADY CHARLOTTE CAMPBELL.
Lady Anne Hamilton.
A YOUNG LADY AND HER MOTHER.
MRS. DALBIAC, a Colonel's wife.
MRS. PRESCOTT, a Captain's wife.
Other English ladies of note and rank.
Madame Grassini and other Ladies of the Opera.

Madame Angiolini, a dancer.
VILLAGE WOMEN.
SOLDIERS' WIVES AND SWEETHEARTS.
A SOLDIER'S DAUGHTER.
....
THE EMPRESS MARIE LOUISE.
The Empress of Austria.
MARIA CAROLINA of Naples.
Queen Hortense.
Laetitia, Madame Bonaparte.
The Princess Pauline.
THE DUCHESS OF MONTEBELLO.
THE COUNTESS OF MONTESQUIOU.
THE COUNTESS OF BRIGNOLE.
Other Ladies-in-Waiting on Marie Louise.

THE EX-EMPRESS JOSEPHINE.
LADIES-IN-WAITING on Josephine.
Another French Lady.
FRENCH MARKET-WOMEN.
A SPANISH LADY.
French and Spanish Women of pleasure.
Continental Citizens' Wives.
Camp-followers.

ACT FIRST

SCENE I

THE BANKS OF THE NIEMEN, NEAR KOWNO

[The foreground is a hillock on a broken upland, seen in evening twilight. On the left, further back, are the dusky forests of Wilkowsky; on the right is the vague shine of a large river.

Emerging from the wood below the eminence appears a shadowy amorphous thing in motion, the central or Imperial column of NAPOLEON'S Grand Army for the invasion of Russia, comprising the corps of OUDINOT, NEY, and DAVOUT, with the Imperial Guard. This, with the right and left columns, makes up the host of nearly half a million, all starting on their march to Moscow.

While the rearmost regiments are arriving, NAPOLEON rides ahead with GENERAL HAXEL and one or two others to reconnoitre the river. NAPOLEON'S horse stumbles and throws him. He picks himself up before he can be helped.]

SPIRIT OF THE YEARS [to Napoleon]
The portent is an ill one, Emperor;

An ancient Roman would retire thereat!

NAPOLEON
Whose voice was that, jarring upon my thought
So insolently?

HAXEL AND OTHERS
Sire, we spoke no word.

NAPOLEON
Then, whoso spake, such portents I defy!

[He remounts. When the reconnoitrers again came back to the foreground of the scene the huge array
of columns is standing quite still, in circles of companies, the captain of each in the middle with a paper
in his hand. He reads from it a proclamation. They quiver emotionally, like leaves stirred by the wind.
NAPOLEON and his staff reascend the hillock, and his own words as repeated to the ranks reach his ears,
while he himself delivers the same address to those about him.

NAPOLEON
Soldiers, wild war is on the board again;
The lifetime-long alliance Russia swore
At Tilsit, for the English realm's undoing,
Is violate beyond refurbishment,
And she intractable and unashamed.
Russia is forced on by fatality:
She cries her destiny must be outwrought,
Meaning at our expense. Does she then dream
We are no more the men of Austerlitz,
With nothing left of our old featfulness?

She offers us the choice of sword or shame;
We have made that choice unhesitatingly!
Then let us forthwith stride the Niemen flood,
Let us bear war into her great gaunt land,
And spread our glory there as otherwhere,
So that a stable peace shall stultify
The evil seed-bearing that Russian wiles
Have nourished upon Europe's choked affairs
These fifty years!

[The midsummer night darkens. They all make their bivouacs and sleep.]

SPIRIT OF THE PITIES
Something is tongued afar.

DISTANT VOICE IN THE WIND
The hostile hatchings of Napoleon's brain
Against our Empire, long have harassed us,

And mangled all our mild amenities.
So, since the hunger for embranglement
That gnaws this man, has left us optionless,
And haled us recklessly to horrid war,
We have promptly mustered our well-hardened hosts,
And, counting on our call to the most High,
Have forthwith set our puissance face to face
Against Napoleon's.—Ranksmen! officers!
You fend your lives, your land, your liberty.
I am with you. Heaven frowns on the aggressor.

SPIRIT IRONIC
Ha! "Liberty" is quaint, and pleases me,
Sounding from such a soil!

[Midsummer-day breaks, and the sun rises on the right, revealing the position clearly. The eminence overlooks for miles the river Niemen, now mirroring the morning rays. Across the river three temporary bridges have been thrown, and towards them the French masses streaming out of the forest descend in three columns.

They sing, shout, fling their shakos in the air and repeat words from the proclamation, their steel and brass flashing in the sun. They narrow their columns as they gain the three bridges, and begin to cross— horse, foot, and artillery.

NAPOLEON has come from the tent in which he has passed the night to the high ground in front, where he stands watching through his glass the committal of his army to the enterprise. DAVOUT, NEY, MURAT, OUDINOT, Generals HAXEL and EBLE, NARBONNE, and others surround him.

It is a day of drowsing heat, and the Emperor draws a deep breath as he shifts his weight from one puffed calf to the other. The light cavalry, the foot, the artillery having passed, the heavy horse now crosses, their glitter outshining the ripples on the stream.

A messenger enters. NAPOLEON reads papers that are brought, and frowns.]

NAPOLEON
The English heads decline to recognize
The government of Joseph, King of Spain,
As that of "the now-ruling dynast";
But only Ferdinand's!—I'll get to Moscow,
And send thence my rejoinder. France shall wage
Another fifty years of wasting war
Before a Bourbon shall remount the throne
Of restless Spain!... [A flash lights his eyes.]

But this long journey now just set a-trip
Is my choice way to India; and 'tis there
That I shall next bombard the British rule.
With Moscow taken, Russia prone and crushed,

To attain the Ganges is simplicity—
Auxiliaries from Tiflis backing me.
Once ripped by a French sword, the scaffolding
Of English merchant-mastership in Ind
Will fall a wreck.... Vast, it is true, must bulk
An Eastern scheme so planned; but I could work it....
Man has, worse fortune, but scant years for war;
I am good for another five!

SPIRIT OF THE PITIES
Why doth he go?—
I see returning in a chattering flock
Bleached skeletons, instead of this array
Invincibly equipped.

SPIRIT OF THE YEARS
I'll show you why.

[The unnatural light before seen usurps that of the sun, bringing into view, like breezes made visible, the films or brain-tissues of the Immanent Will, that pervade all things, ramifying through the whole army, NAPOLEON included, and moving them to Its inexplicable artistries.]

NAPOLEON [with sudden despondency]
That which has worked will work!—Since Lodi Bridge
The force I then felt move me moves me on
Whether I will or no; and oftentimes
Against my better mind.... Why am I here?
—By laws imposed on me inexorably!
History makes use of me to weave her web
To her long while aforetime-figured mesh
And contemplated charactery: no more.
Well, war's my trade; and whencesoever springs
This one in hand, they'll label it with my name!

[The natural light returns and the anatomy of the Will disappears. NAPOLEON mounts his horse and descends in the rear of his host to the banks of the Niemen. His face puts on a saturnine humour, and he hums an air.]

Malbrough s'en va-t-en guerre,
Mironton, mironton, mirontaine;
Malbrough s'en va-t-en guerre,
Ne sait quand reviendra!

[Exeunt NAPOLEON and his staff.]

SPIRIT SINISTER
It is kind of his Imperial Majesty to give me a lead. [Sings.]

Monsieur d'Malbrough est mort,
Mironton, mironton, mirontaine;
Monsieur d'Malbrough est mort,
Est mort et enterre!

[Anon the figure of NAPOLEON, diminished to the aspect of a doll, reappears in front of his suite on the plain below. He rides across the swaying bridge. Since the morning the sky has grown overcast, and its blackness seems now to envelope the retreating array on the other side of the stream. The storm bursts with thunder and lightning, the river turns leaden, and the scene is blotted out by the torrents of rain.]

SCENE II

THE FORD OF SANTA MARTA, SALAMANCA

[We are in Spain, on a July night of the same summer, the air being hot and heavy. In the darkness the ripple of the river Tormes can be heard over the ford, which is near the foreground of the scene.

Against the gloomy north sky to the left, lightnings flash revealing rugged heights in that quarter. From the heights comes to the ear the tramp of soldiery, broke and irregular, as by obstacles in their descent; as yet they are some distance off. On heights to the right hand, on the other side of the river, glimmer the bivouac fires of the French under MARMONT. The lightning quickens, with rolls of thunder, and a few large drops of rain fall.

A sentinel stands close to the ford, and beyond him is the ford-house, a shed open towards the roadway and the spectator. It is lit by a single lantern, and occupied by some half-dozen English dragoons with a sergeant and corporal, who form part of a mounted patrol, their horses being picketed at the entrance. They are seated on a bench, and appear to be waiting with some deep intent, speaking in murmurs only.

The thunderstorm increases till it drowns the noise of the ford and of the descending battalions, making them seem further off than before. The sentinel is about to retreat to the shed when he discerns two female figures in the gloom. Enter MRS. DALBIAC and MRS. PRESCOTT, English officers wives.]

SENTINEL
Where there's war there's women, and where there's women there's trouble! [Aloud] Who goes there?

MRS. DALBIAC
We must reveal who we are, I fear [to her companion]. Friends!
[to sentinel].

SENTINEL
Advance and give the countersign.

MRS. DALBIAC
Oh, but we can't!

SENTINEL

Consequent which, you must retreat. By Lord Wellington's strict regulations, women of loose character are to be excluded from the lines for moral reasons, namely, that they are often employed by the enemy as spies.

MRS. PRESCOTT
Dear good soldier, we are English ladies benighted, having mistaken our way back to Salamanca, and we want shelter from the storm.

MRS. DALBIAC
If it is necessary I will say who we are.—I am Mrs. Dalbiac, wife of the Lieutenant-Colonel of the Fourth Light Dragoons, and this lady is the wife of Captain Prescott of the Seventh Fusileers. We went out to Christoval to look for our husbands, but found the army had moved.

SENTINEL [incredulously]
"Wives!" Oh, not to-day! I have heard such titles of courtesy afore; but they never shake me. "W" begins other female words than "wives!"—You'll have trouble, good dames, to get into Salamanca to-night. You'll be challenged all the way down, and shot without clergy if you can't give the countersign.

MRS. PRESCOTT
Then surely you'll tell us what it is, good kind man!

SENTINEL
Well—have ye earned enough to pay for knowing? Government wage is poor pickings for watching here in the rain. How much can ye stand?

MRS. DALBIAC
Half-a-dozen pesetas.

SENTINEL
Very well, my dear. I was always tender-hearted. Come along. [They advance and hand the money.] The pass to-night is "Melchester Steeple." That will take you into the town when the weather clears. You won't have to cross the ford. You can get temporary shelter in the shed there.

[As the ladies move towards the shed the tramp of the infantry draws near the ford, which the downfall has made to purl more boisterously. The twain enter the shed, and the dragoons look up inquiringly.]

MRS. DALBIAC [to dragoons]
The French are luckier than you are, men. You'll have a wet advance across this ford, but they have a dry retreat by the bridge at Alba.

SERGEANT OF PATROL [starting from a doze]
The moustachies a dry retreat? Not they, my dear. A Spanish garrison is in the castle that commands the bridge at Alba.

MRS. DALBIAC
A peasant told us, if we understood rightly, that he saw the Spanish withdraw, and the enemy place a garrison there themselves.

[The sergeant hastily calls up two troopers, who mount and ride off with the intelligence.]

SERGEANT
You've done us a good turn, it is true, darlin'. Not that Lord Wellington will believe it when he gets the news.... Why, if my eyes don't deceive me, ma'am, that's Colonel Dalbiac's lady!

MRS. DALBIAC
Yes, sergeant. I am over here with him, as you have heard, no doubt, and lodging in Salamanca. We lost our way, and got caught in the storm, and want shelter awhile.

SERGEANT
Certainly, ma'am. I'll give you an escort back as soon as the division has crossed and the weather clears.

MRS. PRESCOTT [anxiously]
Have you heard, sergeant, if there's to be a battle to-morrow?

SERGEANT
Yes, ma'am. Everything shows it.

MRS. DAIBIAC [to MRS. PRESCOTT]
Our news would have passed us in. We have wasted six pesetas.

MRS. PRESCOTT [mournfully]
I don't mind that so much as that I have brought the children from
Ireland. This coming battle frightens me!

SPIRIT OF THE YEARS
This is her prescient pang of widowhood.
Ere Salamanca clang to-morrow's close
She'll find her consort stiff among the slain!

[The infantry regiments now reach the ford. The storm increases in strength, the stream flows more furiously; yet the columns of foot enter it and begin crossing. The lightning is continuous; the faint lantern in the ford-house is paled by the sheets of fire without, which flap round the bayonets of the crossing men and reflect upon the foaming torrent.]

CHORUS OF THE PITIES [aerial music]
The skies fling flame on this ancient land!
And drenched and drowned is the burnt blown sand
That spreads its mantle of yellow-grey
Round old Salmantica to-day;
While marching men come, band on band,
Who read not as a reprimand
To mortal moils that, as 'twere planned
In mockery of their mimic fray,
The skies fling flame.

Since sad Coruna's desperate stand
Horrors unsummed, with heavy hand,
Have smitten such as these! But they
Still headily pursue their way,
Though flood and foe confront them, and
The skies fling flame.

[The whole of the English division gets across by degrees, and their invisible tramp is heard ascending the opposite heights as the lightnings dwindle and the spectacle disappears.]

SCENE III

THE FIELD OF SALAMANCA

[The battlefield—an undulating and sandy expanse—is lying under the sultry sun of a July afternoon. In the immediate left foreground rises boldly a detached dome-like hill known as the Lesser Arapeile, now held by English troops. Further back, and more to the right, rises another and larger hill of the kind—the Greater Arapeile; this is crowned with French artillery in loud action, and the French marshal, MARMONT, Duke of RAGUSA, stands there. Further to the right, in the same plane, stretch the divisions of the French army. Still further to the right, in the distance, on the Ciudad Rodrigo highway, a cloud of dust denotes the English baggage-train seeking security in that direction. The city of Salamanca itself, and the river Tormes on which it stands, are behind the back of the spectator.

On the summit of the lesser hill, close at hand, WELLINGTON, glass at eye, watches the French division under THOMIERE, which has become separated from the centre of the French army. Round and near him are aides and other officers, in animated conjecture on MARMONT'S intent, which appears to be a move on the Ciudad Rodrigo road aforesaid, under the impression that the English are about to retreat that way.

The English commander descends from where he was standing to a nook under a wall, where a meal is roughly laid out. Some of his staff are already eating there. WELLINGTON takes a few mouthfuls without sitting down, walks back again, and looks through his glass at the battle as before. Balls from the French artillery fall around. Enter his aide-de-camp, FITZROY SOMERSET.]

FITZROY SOMERSET [hurriedly]
The French make movements of grave consequence—
Extending to the left in mass, my lord.

WELLINGTON
I have just perceived as much; but not the cause.

[He regards longer.]

Marmont's good genius is deserting him!

[Shutting up his glass with a snap, WELLINGTON calls several aides and despatches them down the hill. He goes back behind the wall and takes some more mouthfuls.]

By God, Fitzroy, if we shan't do it now!
[to SOMERSET].
Mon cher Alava, Marmont est perdu!
[to his SPANISH ATTACHE].

FITZROY SOMERSET
Thinking we mean to attack on him,
He schemes to swoop on our retreating-line.

WELLINGTON
Ay; and to cloak it by this cannonade.
With that in eye he has bundled leftwardly
Thomiere's division; mindless that thereby
His wing and centre's mutual maintenance
Has gone, and left a yawning vacancy.
So be it. Good. His laxness is our luck!

[As a result of the orders sent off by the aides, several British divisions advance across the French front on the Greater Arapeile and elsewhere. The French shower bullets into them; but an English brigade under PACK assails the nearer French on the Arapeile, now beginning to cannonade the English in the hollows beneath.

Light breezes blow toward the French, and they get in their faces the dust-clouds and smoke from the masses of English in motion, and a powerful sun in their eyes.

MARMONT and his staff are sitting on the top of the Greater Arapeile only half a cannon-shot from WELLINGTON on the Lesser; and, like WELLINGTON, he is gazing through his glass.

SPIRIT OF RUMOUR
Appearing to behold the full-mapped mind
Of his opponent, Marmont arrows forth
Aide after aide towards the forest's rim,
To spirit on his troops emerging thence,
And prop the lone division Thomiere,
For whose recall his voice has rung in vain.
Wellington mounts and seeks out Pakenham,
Who pushes to the arena from the right,
And, spurting to the left of Marmont's line,
Shakes Thomiere with lunges leonine.

When the manoeuvre's meaning hits his sense,
Marmont hies hotly to the imperilled place,
Where see him fall, sore smitten.—Bonnet rides
And dons the burden of the chief command,
Marking dismayed the Thomiere column there

Shut up by Pakenham like bellows-folds
Against the English Fourth and Fifth hard by;
And while thus crushed, Dragoon-Guards and Dragoons,
Under Le Marchant's hands [of Guernsey he],
Are launched upon them by Sir Stapleton,
And their scathed files are double-scathed anon.

Cotton falls wounded. Pakenham's bayoneteers Shape for the charge from column into rank;
And Thomiere finds death thereat point-blank!

SEMICHORUS I OF THE PITIES [aerial music]
In fogs of dust the cavalries hoof the ground;
Their prancing squadrons shake the hills around:
Le Marchant's heavies bear with ominous bound
Against their opposites!

SEMICHORUS II
A bullet crying along the cloven air
Gouges Le Marchant's groin and rankles there;
In Death's white sleep he soon joins Thomiere,
And all he has fought for, quits!

[In the meantime the battle has become concentrated in the middle hollow, and WELLINGTON descends thither from the English Arapeile.

The fight grows fiercer. COLE and LEITH now fall wounded; then BERESFORD, who directs the Portuguese, is struck down and borne away. On the French side fall BONNET who succeeded MARMONT in command, MANNE, CLAUSEL, and FEREY, the last hit mortally.

Their disordered main body retreats into the forest and disappears; and just as darkness sets in, the English stand alone on the crest, the distant plain being lighted only by musket-flashes from the vanquishing enemy. In the close foreground vague figures on horseback are audible in the gloom.

VOICE OF WELLINGTON
I thought they looked as they'd be scurrying soon!

VOICE OF AN AIDE
Foy bears into the wood in middling trim;
Maucune strikes out for Alba-Castle bridge.

VOICE OF WELLINGTON
Speed the pursuit, then, towards the Huerta ford;
Their only scantling of escape lies there;
The river coops them semicircle-wise,
And we shall have them like a swathe of grass
Within a sickle's curve!

VOICE OF AIDE

Too late, my lord.
They are crossing by the aforesaid bridge at Alba.

VOICE OF WELLINGTON
Impossible. The guns of Carlos rake it
Sheer from the castle walls.

VOICE OF AIDE
Tidings have sped
Just now therefrom, to this undreamed effect:
That Carlos has withdrawn the garrison:
The French command the Alba bridge themselves!

VOICE OF WELLINGTON
Blast him, he's disobeyed his orders, then!
How happened this? How long has it been known?

VOICE OF AIDE
Some ladies some few hours have rumoured it,
But unbelieved.

VOICE OF WELLINGTON
Well, what's done can't be undone....
By God, though, they've just saved themselves thereby
From capture to a man!

VOICE OF A GENERAL
We've not struck ill,
Despite this slip, my lord.... And have you heard
That Colonel Dalbiac's wife rode in the charge
Behind her spouse to-day?

VOICE OF WELLINGTON
Did she though: did she!
Why that must be Susanna, whom I know—
A Wessex woman, blithe, and somewhat fair....
Not but great irregularities
Arise from such exploits.—And was it she
I noticed wandering to and fro below here,
Just as the French retired?

VOICE OF ANOTHER OFFICER
Ah no, my lord.
That was the wife of Prescott of the Seventh,
Hoping beneath the heel of hopelessness,
As these young women will!—Just about sunset
She found him lying dead and bloody there,
And in the dusk we bore them both away. (18)

VOICE OF WELLINGTON
Well, I'm damned sorry for her. Though I wish
The women-folk would keep them to the rear:
Much awkwardness attends their pottering round!

[The talking shapes disappear, and as the features of the field grow undistinguishable the comparative quiet is broken by gay notes from guitars and castanets in the direction of the city, and other sounds of popular rejoicing at Wellington's victory. People come dancing out from the town, and the merry-making continues till midnight, when it ceases, and darkness and silence prevail everywhere.]

SEMICHORUS I OF THE YEARS [aerial music]
What are Space and Time? A fancy!—
Lo, by Vision's necromancy
Muscovy will now unroll;
Where for cork and olive-tree
Starveling firs and birches be.

SEMICHORUS II
Though such features lie afar
From events Peninsular,
These, amid their dust and thunder,
Form with those, as scarce asunder,
Parts of one compacted whole.

CHORUS
Marmont's aide, then, like a swallow
Let us follow, follow, follow,
Over hill and over hollow,
Past the plains of Teute and Pole!

[There is semblance of a sound in the darkness as of a rushing through the air.]

SCENE IV

THE FIELD OF BORODINO

[Borodino, seventy miles west of Moscow, is revealed in a bird's-eye view from a point above the position of the French Grand Army, advancing on the Russian capital.

We are looking east, towards Moscow and the army of Russia, which bars the way thither. The sun of latter summer, sinking behind our backs, floods the whole prospect, which is mostly wild, uncultivated land with patches of birch-trees. NAPOLEON'S army has just arrived on the scene, and is making its bivouac for the night, some of the later regiments not having yet come up. A dropping fire of musketry from skirmishers ahead keeps snapping through the air. The Emperor's tent stands in a ravine in the foreground amid the squares of the Old Guard. Aides and other officers are chatting outside.

Enter NAPOLEON, who dismounts, speaks to some of his suite, and disappears inside his tent.. An interval follows, during which the sun dips.

Enter COLONEL FABVRIER, aide-de-camp of MARMONT, just arrived from Spain. An officer-in-waiting goes into NAPOLEON'S tent to announce FABVRIER, the Colonel meanwhile talking to those outside.]

AN AIDE
Important tidings thence, I make no doubt?

FABVRIER
Marmont repulsed on Salamanca field,
And well-nigh slain, is the best tale I bring!

[A silence. A coughing heard in NAPOLEON'S tent.]

Whose rheumy throat distracts the quiet so?

AIDE
The Emperor's. He is thus the livelong day.

[COLONEL FABVRIER is shown into the tent. An interval. Then the husky accents of NAPOLEON within, growing louder and louder.]

VOICE OF NAPOLEON
If Marmont—so I gather from these lines—
Had let the English and the Spanish be,
They would have bent from Salamanca back,
Offering no battle, to our profiting!
We should have been delivered this disaster,
Whose bruit will harm us more than aught besides
That has befallen in Spain!

VOICE OF FABVRIER
I fear so, sire.

VOICE OF NAPOLEON
He forced a conflict, to cull laurel crowns
Before King Joseph should arrive to share them!

VOICE OF FABVRIER
The army's ardour for your Majesty,
Its courage, its devotion to your cause,
Cover a myriad of the Marshal's sins.

VOICE OF NAPOLEON
Why gave he battle without biddance, pray,
From the supreme commander? Here's the crime

Of insubordination, root of woes!...
The time well chosen, and the battle won,
The English succours there had sidled off,
And their annoy in the Peninsula
Embarrassed us no more. Behoves it me,
Some day, to face this Wellington myself!
Marmont too plainly is no match for him....
Thus he goes on: "To have preserved command
I would with joy have changed this early wound
For foulest mortal stroke at fall of day.
One baleful moment damnified the fruit
Of six weeks' wise strategics, whose result
Had loomed so certain!"—[Satirically] Well, we've but his word
As to their wisdom! To define them thus
Would not have struck me but for his good prompting!...
No matter: On Moskowa's banks to-morrow
I'll mend his faults upon the Arapeile.
I'll see how I can treat this Russian horde
Which English gold has brought together here
From the four corners of the universe....
Adieu. You'd best go now and take some rest.

[FABVRIER reappears from the tent and goes. Enter DE BAUSSET.]

DE BAUSSET
The box that came—has it been taken in?

AN OFFICER
Yes, General 'Tis laid behind a screen
In the outer tent. As yet his Majesty
Has not been told of it.

[DE BAUSSET goes into the tent. After an interval of murmured talk an exclamation bursts from the EMPEROR. In a few minutes he appears at the tent door, a valet following him bearing a picture. The EMPEROR'S face shows traces of emotion.]

NAPOLEON
Bring out a chair for me to poise it on.

[Re-enter DE BAUSSET from the tent with a chair.]

They all shall see it. Yes, my soldier-sons
Must gaze upon this son of mine own house
In art's presentment! It will cheer their hearts.
That's a good light—just so.

[He is assisted by DE BAUSSET to set up the picture in the chair. It is a portrait of the young King of Rome playing at cup-and-ball being represented as the globe. The officers standing near are attracted round, and then the officers and soldiers further back begin running up, till there is a great crowd.]

Let them walk past,
So that they see him all. The Old Guard first.

[The Old Guard is summoned, and marches past surveying the picture; then other regiments.]

SOLDIERS
The Emperor and the King of Rome for ever!

[When they have marched past and withdrawn, and DE BAUSSET has taken away the picture, NAPOLEON prepares to re-enter his tent. But his attention is attracted to the Russians. He regards them through his glass. Enter BESSIERES and RAPP.]

NAPOLEON
What slow, weird ambulation do I mark,
Rippling the Russian host?

BESSIERES
A progress, sire,
Of all their clergy, vestmented, who bear
An image, said to work strange miracles.

[NAPOLEON watches. The Russian ecclesiastics pass through the regiments, which are under arms, bearing the icon and other religious insignia. The Russian soldiers kneel before it.]

NAPOLEON
Ay! Not content to stand on their own strength,
They try to hire the enginry of Heaven.
I am no theologian, but I laugh
That men can be so grossly logicless,
When war, defensive or aggressive either,
Is in its essence pagan, and opposed
To the whole gist of Christianity!

BESSIERES
'Tis to fanaticize their courage, sire.

NAPOLEON
Better they'd wake up old Kutuzof.—Rapp,
What think you of to-morrow?

RAPP
Victory;
But, sire, a bloody one!

NAPOLEON
So I foresee.

[The scene darkens, and the fires of the bivouacs shine up ruddily, those of the French near at hand, those of the Russians in a long line across the mid-distance, and throwing a flapping glare into the heavens. As the night grows stiller the ballad-singing and laughter from the French mixes with a slow singing of psalms from their adversaries.

The two multitudes lie down to sleep, and all is quiet but for the sputtering of the green wood fires, which, now that the human tongues are still, seem to hold a conversation of their own.]

SCENE V

THE SAME

[The prospect lightens with dawn, and the sun rises red. The spacious field of battle is now distinct, its ruggedness being bisected by the great road from Smolensk to Moscow, which runs centrally from beneath the spectator to the furthest horizon. The field is also crossed by the stream Kalotcha, flowing from the right-centre foreground to the left-centre background, thus forming an "X" with the road aforesaid, intersecting it in mid-distance at the village of Borodino.

Behind this village the Russians have taken their stand in close masses. So stand also the French, who have in their centre the Shevardino redoubt beyond the Kalotcha. Here NAPOLEON, in his usual glue-grey uniform, white waistcoat, and white leather breeches, chooses his position with BERTHIER and other officers of his suite.]

DUMB SHOW
It is six o'clock, and the firing of a single cannon on the French side proclaims that the battle is beginning. There is a roll of drums, and the right-centre masses, glittering in the level shine, advance under NEY and DAVOUT and throw themselves on the Russians, here defended by redoubts.

The French enter the redoubts, whereupon a slim, small man, GENERAL BAGRATION, brings across a division from the Russian right and expels them resolutely.

Semenovskoye is a commanding height opposite the right of the French, and held by the Russians. Cannon and columns, infantry and cavalry, assault it by tens of thousands, but cannot take it.

Aides gallop through the screeching shot and haze of smoke and dust between NAPOLEON and his various marshals. The Emperor walks about, looks through his glass, goes to a camp-stool, on which he sits down, and drinks glasses of spirits and hot water to relieve his still violent cold, as may be discovered from his red eyes, raw nose, rheumatic manner when he moves, and thick voice in giving orders.

SPIRIT OF THE PITIES
So he fulfils the inhuman antickings
He thinks imposed upon him.... What says he?

SPIRIT OF RUMOUR
He says it is the sun of Austerlitz!

The Russians, so far from being driven out of their redoubts, issue from them towards the French. But they have to retreat, BAGRATION and his Chief of Staff being wounded. NAPOLEON sips his grog hopefully, and orders a still stronger attack on the great redoubt in the centre.

It is carried out. The redoubt becomes the scene of a huge massacre. In other parts of the field also the action almost ceases to be a battle, and takes the form of wholesale butchery by the thousand, now advantaging one side, now the other.

SPIRIT OF THE YEARS
Thus do the mindless minions of the spell
In mechanized enchantment sway and show
A Will that wills above the will of each,
Yet but the will of all conjunctively;
A fabric of excitement, web of rage,
That permeates as one stuff the weltering whole.

SPIRIT OF THE PITIES
The ugly horror grossly regnant here
Wakes even the drowsed half-drunken Dictator
To all its vain uncouthness!

SPIRIT OF RUMOUR
Murat cries
That on this much-anticipated day
Napoleon's genius flags inoperative.

The firing from the top of the redoubt has ceased. The French have got inside. The Russians retreat upon their rear, and fortify themselves on the heights there. PONIATOWSKI furiously attacks them. But the French are worn out, and fall back to their station before the battle. So the combat dies resultlessly away. The sun sets, and the opposed and exhausted hosts sink to lethargic repose. NAPOLEON enters his tent in the midst of his lieutenants, and night descends.

SHADE OF THE EARTH
The fumes of nitre and the reek of gore
Make my airs foul and fulsome unto me!

SPIRIT IRONIC
The natural nausea of a nurse, dear Dame.

SPIRIT OF RUMOUR
Strange: even within that tent no notes of joy
Throb as at Austerlitz! [signifying Napoleon's tent].

SPIRIT OF THE PITIES

But mark that roar—
A mash of men's crazed cries entreating mates
To run them through and end their agony;
Boys calling on their mothers, veterans
Blaspheming God and man. Those shady shapes
Are horses, maimed in myriads, tearing round
In maddening pangs, the harnessings they wear
Clanking discordant jingles as they tear!

SPIRIT OF THE YEARS
It is enough. Let now the scene be closed.
The night thickens.

SCENE VI

MOSCOW

[The foreground is an open place amid the ancient irregular streets of the city, which disclose a jumble
of architectural styles, the Asiatic prevailing over the European. A huge triangular white-walled fortress
rises above the churches and coloured domes on a hill in the background, the central feature of which is
a lofty tower with a gilded cupola, the Ivan Tower. Beneath the battlements of this fortress the Moskva
River flows.

An unwonted rumbling of wheels proceeds from the cobble-stoned streets, accompanied by an
incessant cracking of whips.]

DUMB SHOW
Travelling carriages, teams, and waggons, laden with pictures, carpets, glass, silver, china, and
fashionable attire, are rolling out of the city, followed by foot-passengers in streams, who carry their
most precious possessions on their shoulders. Others bear their sick relatives, caring nothing for their
goods, and mothers go laden with their infants. Others drive their cows, sheep, and goats, causing
much obstruction. Some of the populace, however, appear apathetic and bewildered, and stand in
groups asking questions.

A thin man with piercing eyes gallops about and gives stern orders.

SPIRIT OF THE PITIES
Whose is the form seen ramping restlessly,
Geared as a general, keen-eyed as a kite,
Mid this mad current of close-filed confusion;
High-ordering, smartening progress in the slow,
And goading those by their own thoughts o'er-goaded;
Whose emissaries knock at every door
In rhythmal rote, and groan the great events
The hour is pregnant with?

SPIRIT OF THE YEARS
Rostopchin he,
The city governor, whose name will ring
Far down the forward years uncannily!

SPIRIT OF RUMOUR
His arts are strange, and strangely do they move him:—
To store the stews with stuffs inflammable,
To bid that pumps be wrecked, captives enlarged
And primed with brands for burning, are the intents
His warnings to the citizens outshade!

When the bulk of the populace has passed out eastwardly the Russian army retreating from Borodino also passes through the city into the country beyond without a halt. They mostly move in solemn silence, though many soldiers rush from their ranks and load themselves with spoil.

When they are got together again and have marched out, there goes by on his horse a strange scarred old man with a foxy look, a swollen neck and head and a hunched figure. He is KUTUZOF, surrounded by his lieutenants. Away in the distance by other streets and bridges with other divisions pass in like manner GENERALS BENNIGSEN, BARCLAY DE TOLLY, DOKHTOROF, the mortally wounded BAGRATION in a carriage, and other generals, all in melancholy procession one way, like autumnal birds of passage. Then the rear-guard passes under MILORADOVITCH.

Next comes a procession of another kind.

A long string of carts with wounded men is seen, which trails out of the city behind the army. Their clothing is soiled with dried blood, and the bandages that enwrap them are caked with it.

The greater part of this migrant multitude takes the high road to Vladimir.

SCENE VII

THE SAME. OUTSIDE THE CITY

[A hill forms the foreground, called the Hill of Salutation, near the Smolensk road.

Herefrom the city appears as a splendid panorama, with its river, its gardens, and its curiously grotesque architecture of domes and spires. It is the peacock of cities to Western eyes, its roofs twinkling in the rays of the September sun, amid which the ancient citadel of the Tsars—the Kremlin—forms a centre-piece.

There enter on the hill at a gallop NAPOLEON, MURAT, EUGENE, NEY, DARU, and the rest of the Imperial staff. The French advance-guard is drawn up in order of battle at the foot of the hill, and the long columns of the Grand Army stretch far in the rear. The Emperor and his marshals halt, and gaze at Moscow.]

NAPOLEON
Ha! There she is at last. And it was time.

[He looks round upon his army, its numbers attenuated to one-fourth of those who crossed the Niemen so joyfully.]

Yes: it was time.... NOW what says Alexander!

DARU
This is a foil to Salamanca, sire!

DAVOUT
What scores of bulbous church-tops gild the sky!
Souls must be rotten in this region, sire,
To need so much repairing!

NAPOLEON
Ay—no doubt....
Prithee march briskly on, to check disorder,
[to Murat].
Hold word with the authorities forthwith,
[to Durasnel].
Tell them that they may swiftly swage their fears,
Safe in the mercy I by rule extend
To vanquished ones. I wait the city keys,
And will receive the Governor's submission
With courtesy due. Eugene will guard the gate
To Petersburg there leftward. You, Davout,
The gate to Smolensk in the centre here
Which we shall enter by.

VOICES OF ADVANCE-GUARD
Moscow! Moscow!
This, this is Moscow city. Rest at last!

[The words are caught up in the rear by veterans who have entered every capital in Europe except London, and are echoed from rank to rank. There is a far-extended clapping of hands, like the babble of waves, and companies of foot run in disorder towards high ground to behold the spectacle, waving their shakos on their bayonets.

The army now marches on, and NAPOLEON and his suite disappear citywards from the Hill of Salutation.

The day wanes ere the host has passed and dusk begins to prevail, when tidings reach the rear-guard that cause dismay. They have been sent back lip by lip from the front.]

SPIRIT IRONIC
An anticlimax to Napoleon's dream!

SPIRIT OF RUMOUR
They say no governor attends with keys
To offer his submission gracefully.
The streets are solitudes, the houses sealed,
And stagnant silence reigns, save where intrudes
The rumbling of their own artillery wheels,
And their own soldiers' measured tramp along.
"Moscow deserted? What a monstrous thing!"—
He shrugs his shoulders soon, contemptuously;
"This, then is how Muscovy fights!" cries he.

Meanwhile Murat has reached the Kremlin gates,
And finds them closed against him. Battered these,
The fort reverberates vacant as the streets
But for some grinning wretches gaoled there.
Enchantment seems to sway from quay to keep,
And lock commotion in a century's sleep.

[NAPOLEON, reappearing in front of the city, follows MURAT, and is again lost to view. He has entered the Kremlin. An interval. Something becomes visible on the summit of the Ivan Tower.]

CHORUS OF RUMOURS [aerial music]
Mark you thereon a small lone figure gazing
Upon his hard-gained goal? It is He!
The startled crows, their broad black pinions raising,
Forsake their haunts, and wheel disquietedly.

[The scene slowly darkens. Midnight hangs over the city. In blackness to the north of where the Kremlin stands appears what at first seems a lurid, malignant star. It waxes larger. Almost simultaneously a north-east wind rises, and the light glows and sinks with the gusts, proclaiming a fire, which soon grows large enough to irradiate the fronts of adjacent buildings, and to show that it is creeping on towards the Kremlin itself, the walls of that fortress which face the flames emerging from their previous shade.

The fire can be seen breaking out also in numerous other quarters. All the conflagrations increase, and become, as those at first detached group themselves together, one huge furnace, whence streamers of flame reach up to the sky, brighten the landscape far around, and show the houses as if it were day. The blaze gains the Kremlin, and licks its walls, but does not kindle it. Explosions and hissings are constantly audible, amid which can be fancied cries and yells of people caught in the combustion. Large pieces of canvas aflare sail away on the gale like balloons. Cocks crow, thinking it sunrise, ere they are burnt to death.]

SCENE VIII

THE SAME. THE INTERIOR OF THE KREMLIN

[A chamber containing a bed on which NAPOLEON has been lying. It is not yet daybreak, and the flapping light of the conflagration without shines in at the narrow windows.

NAPOLEON is discovered dressed, but in disorder and unshaven. He is walking up and down the room in agitation. There are present CAULAINCOURT, BESSIERES, and many of the marshals of his guard, who stand in silent perplexity.]

NAPOLEON [sitting down on the bed]
No: I'll not go! It is themselves who have done it.
My God, they are Scythians and barbarians still!

[Enter MORTIER [just made Governor].]

MORTIER
Sire, there's no means of fencing with the flames.
My creed is that these scurvy Muscovites
Knowing our men's repute for recklessness,
Have fired the town, as if 'twere we had done it,
As by our own crazed act!

[GENERAL LARIBOISIERE, and aged man, enters and approaches NAPOLEON.]

LARIBOISIERE
The wind swells higher!
Will you permit one so high-summed in years,
One so devoted, sire, to speak his mind?
It is that your long lingering here entails
Much risk for you, your army, and ourselves,
In the embarrassment it throws on us
While taking steps to seek security,
By hindering venturous means.

[Enter MURAT, PRINCE EUGENE, and the PRINCE OF NEUFCHATEL.]

MURAT
There is no choice
But leaving, sire. Enormous bulks of powder
Lie housed beneath us; and outside these panes
A park of our artillery stands unscreened.

NAPOLEON [saturninely]
What have I won I disincline to cede!

VOICE OF A GUARD [without]
The Kremlin is aflame!

[The look at each other. Two officers of NAPOLEON'S guard and an interpreter enter, with one of the Russian military police as a prisoner.]

FIRST OFFICER
We have caught this man
Firing the Kremlin: yea, in the very act!
It is extinguished temporarily,
We know not for how long.

NAPOLEON
Inquire of him
What devil set him on. [They inquire.]

SECOND OFFICER
The governor,
He says; the Count Rostopchin, sire.

NAPOLEON
So! Even the ancient Kremlin is not sanct
From their infernal scheme! Go, take him out;
Make him a quick example to the rest.

[Exeunt guard with their prisoner to the court below, whence a musket-volley resounds in a few minutes. Meanwhile the flames pop and spit more loudly, and the window-panes of the room they stand in crack and fall in fragments.]

Incendiarism afoot, and we unware
Of what foul tricks may follow, I will go.
Outwitted here, we'll march on Petersburg,
The Devil if we won't!

[The marshals murmur and shake their heads.]

BESSIERES
Your pardon, sire,
But we are all convinced that weather, time,
Provisions, roads, equipment, mettle, mood,
Serve not for such a perilous enterprise.

[NAPOLEON remains in gloomy silence. Enter BERTHIER.]

NAPOLEON [apathetically]
Well, Berthier. More misfortunes?

BERTHIER
News is brought,
Sire, of the Russian army's whereabouts.
That fox Kutuzof, after marching east
As if he were conducting his whole force
To Vladimir, when at the Riazan Road

Down-doubled sharply south, and in a curve
Has wheeled round Moscow, making for Kalouga,
To strike into our base, and cut us off.

MURAT
Another reason against Petersburg!
Come what come may, we must defeat that army,
To keep a sure retreat through Smolensk on
To Lithuania.

NAPOLEON [jumping up]
I must act! We'll leave,
Or we shall let this Moscow be our tomb.
May Heaven curse the author of this war—
Ay, him, that Russian minister, self-sold
To England, who fomented it.—'Twas he
Dragged Alexander into it, and me!

[The marshals are silent with looks of incredulity, and Caulaincourt shrugs his shoulders.]

Now no more words; but hear. Eugene and Ney
With their divisions fall straight back upon
The Petersburg and Zwenigarod Roads;
Those of Davout upon the Smolensk route.
I will retire meanwhile to Petrowskoi.
Come, let us go.

[NAPOLEON and the marshals move to the door. In leaving, the Emperor pauses and looks back.]

I fear that this event
Marks the beginning of a train of ills....
Moscow was meant to be my rest,
My refuge, and—it vanishes away!

[Exeunt NAPOLEON, marshals, etc. The smoke grows denser and obscures the scene.]

SCENE IX

THE ROAD FROM SMOLENSKO INTO LITHUANIA

[The season is far advanced towards winter. The point of observation is high amongst the clouds, which, opening and shutting fitfully to the wind, reveal the earth as a confused expanse merely.]

SPIRIT OF THE PITIES
Where are we? And why are we where we are?

SHADE OF THE EARTH
Above a wild waste garden-plot of mine
Nigh bare in this late age, and now grown chill,
Lithuania called by some. I gather not
Why we haunt here, where I can work no charm
Either upon the ground or over it.

SPIRIT OF THE YEARS
The wherefore will unfold. The rolling brume
That parts, and joins, and parts again below us
In ragged restlessness, unscreens by fits
The quality of the scene.

SPIRIT OF THE PITIES
I notice now
Primeval woods, pine, birch—the skinny growths
That can sustain life well where earth affords
But sustenance elsewhere yclept starvation.

SPIRIT OF THE YEARS
And what see you on the far land-verge there,
Labouring from eastward towards our longitude?

SPIRIT OF THE PITIES
An object like a dun-piled caterpillar,
Shuffling its length in painful heaves along,
Hitherward.... Yea, what is this Thing we see
Which, moving as a single monster might,
Is yet not one but many?

SPIRIT OF THE YEARS
Even the Army
Which once was called the Grand; now in retreat
From Moscow's muteness, urged by That within it;
Together with its train of followers—
Men, matrons, babes, in brabbling multitudes.

SPIRIT OF THE PITIES
And why such flight?

SPIRIT OF THE YEARS
Recording Angels, say.

RECORDING ANGEL I [in minor plain-song]
The host has turned from Moscow where it lay,
And Israel-like, moved by some master-sway,
Is made to wander on and waste away!

ANGEL II
By track of Tarutino first it flits;
Thence swerving, strikes at old Jaroslawitz;
The which, accurst by slaughtering swords, it quits.

ANGEL I
Harassed, it treads the trail by which it came,
To Borodino, field of bloodshot fame,
Whence stare unburied horrors beyond name!

ANGEL II
And so and thus it nears Smolensko's walls,
And, stayed its hunger, starts anew its crawls,
Till floats down one white morsel, which appals.

[What has floated down from the sky upon the Army is a flake of snow. Then come another and another, till natural features, hitherto varied with the tints of autumn, are confounded, and all is phantasmal grey and white.

The caterpillar shape still creeps laboriously nearer, but instead, increasing in size by the rules of perspective, it gets more attenuated, and there are left upon the ground behind it minute parts of itself, which are speedily flaked over, and remain as white pimples by the wayside.]

SPIRIT OF THE YEARS
These atoms that drop off are snuffed-out souls
Who are enghosted by the caressing snow.

[Pines rise mournfully on each side of the nearing object; ravens in flocks advance with it overhead, waiting to pick out the eyes of strays who fall. The snowstorm increases, descending in tufts which can hardly be shaken off. The sky seems to join itself to the land. The marching figures drop rapidly, and almost immediately become white grave-mounds.

Endowed with enlarged powers of audition as of vision, we are struck by the mournful taciturnity that prevails. Nature is mute. Save for the incessant flogging of the wind-broken and lacerated horses there are no sounds.

With growing nearness more is revealed. In the glades of the forest, parallel to the French columns, columns of Russians are seen to be moving. And when the French presently reach Krasnoye they are surrounded by packs of cloaked Cossacks, bearing lances like huge needles a dozen feet long. The fore-part of the French army gets through the town; the rear is assaulted by infantry and artillery.]

SPIRIT OF THE PITIES
The strange, one-eyed, white-shakoed, scarred old man,
Ruthlessly heading every onset made,
I seem to recognize.

SPIRIT OF THE YEARS
Kutuzof he:

The ceaselessly-attacked one, Michael Ney;
A pair as stout as thou, Earth, ever hast twinned!
Kutuzof, ten years younger, would extirp
The invaders, and our drama finish here,
With Bonaparte a captive or a corpse.
But he is old; death even has beckoned him;
And thus the so near-seeming happens not.

[NAPOLEON himself can be discerned amid the rest, marching on foot through the snowflakes, in a fur coat and with a stout staff in his hand. Further back NEY is visible with the remains of the rear.

There is something behind the regular columns like an articulated tail, and as they draw on, it shows itself to be a disorderly rabble of followers of both sexes. So the whole miscellany arrives at the foreground, where it is checked by a large river across the track. The soldiers themselves, like the rabble, are in motley raiment, some wearing rugs for warmth, some quilts and curtains, some even petticoats and other women's clothing. Many are delirious from hunger and cold.

But they set about doing what is a necessity for the least hope of salvation, and throw a bridge across the stream.

The point of vision descends to earth, close to the scene of action.]

SCENE X

THE BRIDGE OF THE BERESINA

[The bridge is over the Beresina at Studzianka. On each side of the river are swampy meadows, now hard with frost, while further back are dense forests. Ice floats down the deep black stream in large cakes.]

DUMB SHOW
The French sappers are working up to their shoulders in the water at the building of the bridge. Those so immersed work till, stiffened with ice to immobility, they die from the chill, when others succeed them.

Cavalry meanwhile attempt to swim their horses across, and some infantry try to wade through the stream.

Another bridge is begun hard by, the construction of which advances with greater speed; and it becomes fit for the passage of carriages and artillery.

NAPOLEON is seen to come across to the homeward bank, which is the foreground of the scene. A good portion of the army also, under DAVOUT, NEY, and OUDINOT, lands by degrees on this side. But VICTOR'S corps is yet on the left or Moscow side of the stream, moving toward the bridge, and PARTONNEAUX with the rear-guard, who has not yet crossed, is at Borissow, some way below, where there is an old permanent bridge partly broken.

Enter with speed from the distance the Russians under TCHAPLITZ. More under TCHICHAGOFF enter the scene down the river on the left or further bank, and cross by the old bridge of Borissow. But they are too far from the new crossing to intercept the French as yet.

PLATOFF with his Cossacks next appears on the stage which is to be such a tragic one. He comes from the forest and approaches the left bank likewise. So also does WITTGENSTEIN, who strikes in between the uncrossed VICTOR and PARTONNEAUX. PLATOFF thereupon descends on the latter, who surrenders with the rear-guard; and thus seven thousand more are cut off from the already emaciated Grand Army.

TCHAPLITZ, of TCHICHAGOFF'S division, has meanwhile got round by the old bridge at Borissow to the French side of the new one, and attacks OUDINOT; but he is repulsed with the strength of despair. The French lose a further five thousand in this.

We now look across the river at VICTOR, and his division, not yet over, and still defending the new bridges. WITTGENSTEIN descends upon him; but he holds his ground.

The determined Russians set up a battery of twelve cannon, so as to command the two new bridges, with the confused crowd of soldiers, carriages, and baggage, pressing to cross. The battery discharges into the surging multitude. More Russians come up, and, forming a semicircle round the bridges and the mass of French, fire yet more hotly on them with round shot and canister. As it gets dark the flashes light up the strained faces of the fugitives. Under the discharge and the weight of traffic, the bridge for the artillery gives way, and the throngs upon it roll shrieking into the stream and are drowned.

SEMICHORUS I OF THE PITIES [aerial music]
So loudly swell their shrieks as to be heard above the roar of guns and the wailful wind,
Giving in one brief cry their last wild word on that mock life through which they have harlequined!

SEMICHORUS II
To the other bridge the living heap betakes itself, the weak pushed over by the strong;
They loop together by their clutch like snakes; in knots they are submerged and borne along.

CHORUS
Then women are seen in the waterflow—limply bearing their infants between wizened white arms stretching above; Yea, motherhood, sheerly sublime in her last despairing, and lighting her darkest declension with limitless love.

Meanwhile, TCHICHAGOFF has come up with his twenty-seven thousand men, and falls on OUDINOT, NEY, and the "Sacred Squadron." Altogether we see forty or fifty thousand assailing eighteen thousand half-naked, badly armed wretches, emaciated with hunger and encumbered with several thousands of sick, wounded, and stragglers.

VICTOR and his rear-guard, who have protected the bridges all day, come over themselves at last. No sooner have they done so than the final bridge is set on fire. Those who are upon it burn or drown; those who are on the further side have lost their last chance, and perish either in attempting to wade the stream or at the hands of the Russians.

SEMICHORUS OF THE PITIES [aerial music]

What will be seen in the morning light?
What will be learnt when the spring breaks bright,
And the frost unlocks to the sun's soft sight?

SEMICHORUS II
Death in a thousand motley forms;
Charred corpses hooking each other's arms
In the sleep that defies all war's alarms!

CHORUS
Pale cysts of souls in every stage,
Still bent to embraces of love or rage,—
Souls passed to where History pens no page.

The flames of the burning bridge go out as it consumes to the water's edge, and darkness mantles all,
nothing continuing but the purl of the river and the clickings of floating ice.

SCENE XI

THE OPEN COUNTRY BETWEEN SMORGONI AND WILNA

[The winter is more merciless, and snow continues to fall upon a deserted expanse of unenclosed land in
Lithuania. Some scattered birch bushes merge in a forest in the background.

It is growing dark, though nothing distinguishes where the sun sets. There is no sound except that of a
shuffling of feet in the direction of a bivouac. Here are gathered tattered men like skeletons. Their
noses and ears are frost-bitten, and pus is oozing from their eyes.

These stricken shades in a limbo of gloom are among the last survivors of the French army. Few of them
carry arms. One squad, ploughing through snow above their knees, and with icicles dangling from their
hair that clink like glass-lustres as they walk, go into the birch wood, and are heard chopping. They bring
back boughs, with which they make a screen on the windward side, and contrive to light a fire. With
their swords they cut rashers from a dead horse, and grill them in the flames, using gunpowder for salt
to eat them with. Two others return from a search, with a dead rat and some candle-ends. Their meal
shared, some try to repair their gaping shoes and to tie up their feet, that are chilblained to the bone.

A straggler enters, who whispers to one or two soldiers of the group. A shudder runs through them at
his words.]

FIRST SOLDIER [dazed]
What—gone, do you say? Gone?

STRAGGLER
Yes, I say gone!
He left us at Smorgoni hours ago.
The Sacred Squadron even he has left behind.

By this time he's at Warsaw or beyond,
Full pace for Paris.

SECOND SOLDIER [jumping up wildly]
Gone? How did he go?
No, surely! He could not desert us so!

STRAGGLER
He started in a carriage, with Roustan
The Mameluke on the box: Caulaincourt, too,
Was inside with him. Monton and Duroc
Rode on a sledge behind.—The order bade
That we should not be told it for a while.

[Other soldiers spring up as they realize the news, and stamp hither and thither, impotent with rage, grief, and despair, many in their physical weakness sobbing like children.]

SPIRIT SINISTER
Good. It is the selfish and unconscionable characters who are so much regretted.

STRAGGLER
He felt, or feigned, he ought to leave no longer
A land like Prussia 'twixt himself and home.
There was great need for him to go, he said,
To quiet France, and raise another army
That shall replace our bones.

SEVERAL [distractedly]
Deserted us!
Deserted us!—O, after all our pangs
We shall see France no more!

[Some become insane, and go dancing round. One of them sings.]

MAD SOLDIER'S SONG
I
Ha, for the snow and hoar!
Ho, for our fortune's made!
We can shape our bed without sheets to spread,
And our graves without a spade.
So foolish Life adieu,
And ingrate Leader too.
—Ah, but we loved you true!
Yet—he-he-he! and ho-ho-ho-!—
We'll never return to you.

II
What can we wish for more?

Thanks to the frost and flood
We are grinning crones—thin bags of bones
Who once were flesh and blood.
So foolish Life adieu,
And ingrate Leader too.
—Ah, but we loved you true!
Yet—he-he-he! and ho-ho-ho!—
We'll never return to you.

[Exhausted, they again crouch round the fire. Officers and privates press together for warmth. Other stragglers arrive, and sit at the backs of the first. With the progress of the night the stars come out in unusual brilliancy, Sirius and those in Orion flashing like stilettos; and the frost stiffens.

The fire sinks and goes out; but the Frenchmen do not move. The day dawns, and still they sit on.

In the background enter some light horse of the Russian army, followed by KUTUZOF himself and a few of his staff. He presents a terrible appearance now—bravely serving though slowly dying, his face puffed with the intense cold, his one eye staring out as he sits in a heap in the saddle, his head sunk into his shoulders. The whole detachment pauses at the sight of the French asleep. They shout; but the bivouackers give no sign.

KUTUZOF
Go, stir them up! We slay not sleeping men.

[The Russians advance and prod the French with their lances.]

RUSSIAN OFFICER
Prince, here's a curious picture. They are dead.

KUTUZOF [with indifference]
Oh, naturally. After the snow was down
I marked a sharpening of the air last night.
We shall be stumbling on such frost-baked meat
Most of the way to Wilna.

OFFICER [examining the bodies]
They all sit
As they were living still, but stiff as horns;
And even the colour has not left their cheeks,
Whereon the tears remain in strings of ice.—
It was a marvel they were not consumed:
Their clothes are cindered by the fire in front,
While at their back the frost has caked them hard.

KUTUZOF
'Tis well. So perish Russia's enemies!

[Exeunt KUTUZOF, his staff, and the detachment of horse in the direction of Wilna; and with the advance of day the snow resumes its fall, slowly burying the dead bivouackers.]

SCENE XII

PARIS. THE TUILERIES

[An antechamber to the EMPRESS MARIE LOUISE'S bedroom, at half-past eleven on a December night. The DUCHESS OF MONTEBELLO and another lady-in-waiting are discovered talking to the Empress.]

MARIE LOUISE
I have felt unapt for anything to-night,
And I will now retire.

[She goes into her child's room adjoining.]

DUCHESS OF MONTEBELLO
For some long while
There has come no letter from the Emperor,
And Paris brims with ghastly rumourings
About the far campaign. Not being beloved,
The town is over dull for her alone.

[Re-enter MARIE LOUISE.]

MARIE LOUISE
The King of Rome is sleeping in his cot
Sweetly and safe. Now, ladies, I am going.

[She withdraws. Her tiring-women pass through into her chamber. They presently return and go out. A manservant enters, and bars the window-shutters with numerous bolts. Exit manservant. The Duchess retires. The other lady-in-waiting rises to go into her bedroom, which adjoins that of the Empress.

Men's voices are suddenly heard in the corridor without. The lady-in-waiting pauses with parted lips. The voices grow louder. The lady-in-waiting screams.

MARIE LOUISE hastily re-enters in a dressing-gown thrown over her night-clothes.]

MARIE LOUISE
Great God, what altercation can that be?
I had just verged on sleep when it aroused me!

[A thumping is heard at the door.]

VOICE OF NAPOLEON [without]
Hola! Pray let me in! Unlock the door!

LADY-IN-WAITING
Heaven's mercy on us! What man may it be
At such and hour as this?

MARIE LOUISE
O it is he!

[The lady-in-waiting unlocks the door. NAPOLEON enters, scarcely recognizable, in a fur cloak and hood
over his ears. He throws off the cloak and discloses himself to be in the shabbiest and muddiest attire.
Marie Louise is agitated almost to fainting.]

SPIRIT IRONIC
Is it with fright or joy?

MARIE LOUISE
I scarce believe
What my sight tells me! Home, and in such garb!

[NAPOLEON embraces her.]

NAPOLEON
I have had great work in getting in, my dear!
They failed to recognize me at the gates,
Being sceptical at my poor hackney-coach
And poorer baggage. I had to show my face
In a fierce light ere they would let me pass,
And even then they doubted till I spoke.—
What think you, dear, of such a tramp-like spouse?
[He warms his hands at the fire.]
Ha—it is much more comfortable here
Than on the Russian plains!

MARIE LOUISE [timidly]
You have suffered there?—
Your face is thinner, and has line in it;
No marvel that they did not know you!

NAPOLEON
Yes:
Disasters many and swift have swooped on me!—
Since crossing—ugh!—the Beresina River
I have been compelled to come incognito;
Ay—as a fugitive and outlaw quite.

MARIE LOUISE
We'll thank Heaven, anyhow, that you are safe.
I had gone to bed, and everybody almost!

what, now, do require? Some food of course?

[The child in the adjoining chamber begins to cry, awakened by the loud tones of NAPOLEON.]

NAPOLEON
Ah—that's his little voice! I'll in and see him.

MARIE LOUISE
I'll come with you.

[NAPOLEON and the EMPRESS pass into the other room. The lady-in- waiting calls up yawning servants and gives orders. The servants go to execute them. Re-enter NAPOLEON and MARIE LOUISE. The lady-in-waiting goes out.]

NAPOLEON
I have said it, dear!
All the disasters summed in the bulletin
Shall be repaired.

MARIE LOUISE
And are they terrible?

NAPOLEON
Have you not read the last-sent bulletin,
Dear friend?

MARIE LOUISE
No recent bulletin has come.

NAPOLEON
Ah—I must have outstripped it on the way!

MARIE LOUISE
And where is the Grand Army?

NAPOLEON
Oh—that's gone.

MARIE LOUISE
Gone? But—gone where?

NAPOLEON
Gone all to nothing, dear.

MARIE LOUISE [incredulously]
But some six hundred thousand I saw pass
Through Dresden Russia-wards?

NAPOLEON [flinging himself into a chair]
Well, those men lie—
Or most of them—in layers of bleaching bones
'Twixt here and Moscow.... I have been subdued;
But by the elements; and them alone.
Not Russia, but God's sky has conquered me!
[With an appalled look she sits beside him.]
From the sublime to the ridiculous
There's but a step!—I have been saying it
All through the leagues of my long journey home—
And that step has been passed in this affair!...
Yes, briefly, it is quite ridiculous,
Whichever way you look at it.—Ha, ha!

MARIE LOUISE [simply]
But those six hundred thousand throbbing throats
That cheered me deaf at Dresden, marching east
So full of youth and spirits—all bleached bones—
Ridiculous? Can it be so, dear, to—
Their mothers say?

NAPOLEON [with a twitch of displeasure]
You scarcely understand.
I meant the enterprise, and not its stuff....
I had no wish to fight, nor Alexander,
But circumstance impaled us each on each;
The Genius who outshapes my destinies
Did all the rest! Had I but hit success,
Imperial splendour would have worn a crown
Unmatched in long-scrolled Time!... Well, leave that now.—
What do they know about all this in Paris?

MARIE LOUSE
I cannot say. Black rumours fly and croak
Like ravens through the streets, but come to me
Thinned to the vague!—Occurrences in Spain
Breed much disquiet with these other things.
Marmont's defeat at Salamanca field
Ploughed deep into men's brows. The cafes say
Your troops must clear from Spain.

NAPOLEON
We'll see to that!
I'll find a way to do a better thing;
Though I must have another army first—
Three hundred thousand quite. Fishes as good
Swim in the sea as have come out of it.
But to begin, we must make sure of France,

Disclose ourselves to the good folk of Paris
In daily outing as a family group,
The type and model of domestic bliss
[Which, by the way, we are]. And I intend,
Also, to gild the dome of the Invalides
In best gold leaf, and on a novel pattern.

MARIE LOUISE
To gild the dome, dear? Why?

NAPOLEON
To give them something
To think about. They'll take to it like children,
And argue in the cafes right and left
On its artistic points.—So they'll forget
The woes of Moscow.

[A chamberlain-in-waiting announces supper. MARIE LOUISE and NAPOLEON go out. The room darkens and the scene closes.]

ACT SECOND

SCENE I

THE PLAIN OF VITORIA

[It is the eve of the longest day of the year; also the eve of the battle of Vitoria. The English army in the Peninsula, and their Spanish and Portuguese allies, are bivouacking on the western side of the Plain, about six miles from the town.

On some high ground in the left mid-distance may be discerned the MARQUIS OF WELLINGTON'S tent, with GENERALS HILL, PICTON, PONSONBY, GRAHAM, and others of his staff, going in and out in consultation on the momentous event impending. Near the foreground are some hussars sitting round a fire, the evening being damp; their horses are picketed behind. In the immediate front of the scene are some troop-officers talking.]

FIRST OFFICER
This grateful rest of four-and-twenty hours
Is priceless for our jaded soldiery;
And we have reconnoitred largely, too;
So the slow day will not have slipped in vain.

SECOND OFFICER [looking towards the headquarter tent]
By this time they must nearly have dotted down
The methods of our master-stroke to-morrow:

I have no clear conception of its plan,
Even in its leading lines. What is decided?

FIRST OFFICER
There are outshaping three supreme attacks,
As I decipher. Graham's on the left,
To compass which he crosses the Zadorra,
And turns the enemy's right. On our right, Hill
Will start at once to storm the Puebla crests.
The Chief himself, with us here in the centre,
Will lead on by the bridges Tres-Puentes
Over the ridge there, and the Mendoza bridge
A little further up.—That's roughly it;
But much and wide discretionary power
Is left the generals all.

[The officers walk away, and the stillness increases, so the conversation at the hussars' bivouac, a few
yards further back, becomes noticeable.]

SERGEANT YOUNG (19)
I wonder, I wonder how Stourcastle is looking this summer night, and all the old folks there!

SECOND HUSSAR
You was born there, I think I've heard ye say, Sergeant?

SERGEANT YOUNG
I was. And though I ought not to say it, as father and mother are living there still, 'tis a dull place at
times. Now Budmouth-Regis was exactly to my taste when we were there with the Court that summer,
and the King and Queen a-wambling about among us like the most everyday old man and woman you
ever see. Yes, there was plenty going on, and only a pretty step from home. Altogether we had a fine
time!

THIRD HUSSAR
You walked with a girl there for some weeks, Sergeant, if my memory serves?

SERGEANT YOUNG
I did. And a pretty girl 'a was. But nothing came on't. A month afore we struck camp she married a
tallow-chandler's dipper of Little Nicholas Lane. I was a good deal upset about it at the time. But one
gets over things!

SECOND HUSSAR
'Twas a low taste in the hussy, come to that.—Howsomever, I agree about Budmouth. I never had
pleasanter times than when we lay there. You had a song on it, Sergeant, in them days, if I don't
mistake?

SERGEANT YOUNG
I had; and have still. 'Twas made up when we left by our bandmaster that used to conduct in front of
Gloucester Lodge at the King's Mess every afternoon.

[The Sergeant is silent for a minute, then suddenly bursts into melody.]

SONG "BUDMOUTH DEARS"
I
When we lay where Budmouth Beach is,
O, the girls were fresh as peaches,
With their tall and tossing figures and their eyes of blue and brown!
And our hearts would ache with longing
As we paced from our sing-songing,
With a smart CLINK! CLINK! up the Esplanade and down

II
They distracted and delayed us
By the pleasant pranks they played us,
And what marvel, then, if troopers, even of regiments of renown,
On whom flashed those eyes divine, O,
Should forget the countersign, O,
As we tore CLINK! CLINK! back to camp above the town.

III
Do they miss us much, I wonder,
Now that war has swept us sunder,
And we roam from where the faces smile to where the faces frown?
And no more behold the features
Of the fair fantastic creatures,
And no more CLINK! CLINK! past the parlours of the town?

IV
Shall we once again there meet them?
Falter fond attempts to greet them?
Will the gay sling-jacket (1) glow again beside the muslin gown?—
Will they archly quiz and con us
With a sideways glance upon us,
While our spurs CLINK! CLINK! up the Esplanade and down?

[Applause from the other hussars. More songs are sung, the night gets darker, the fires go out, and the camp sleeps.]

SCENE II

THE SAME, FROM THE PUEBLA HEIGHTS

[It is now day; but a summer fog pervades the prospect. Behind the fog is heard the roll of bass and tenor drums and the clash of cymbals, with notes of the popular march "The Downfall of Paris."

By degrees the fog lifts, and the Plain is disclosed. From this elevation, gazing north, the expanse looks like the palm of a monstrous right hand, a little hollowed, some half-dozen miles across, wherein the ball of the thumb is roughly represented by heights to the east, on which the French centre has gathered; the "Mount of Mars" and the "Moon" [the opposite side of the palm] by the position of the English on the left or west of the plain; and the "Line of Life" by the Zadorra, an unfordable river running from the town down the plain, and dropping out of it through a pass in the Puebla Heights to the south, just beneath our point of observation—that is to say, toward the wrist of the supposed hand. The left of the English army under GRAHAM would occupy the "mounts" at the base of the fingers; while the bent finger-tips might represent the Cantabrian Hills beyond the plain to the north or back of the scene.

From the aforesaid stony crests of Puebla the white town and church towers of Vitoria can be descried on a slope to the right-rear of the field of battle. A warm rain succeeds the fog for a short while, bringing up the fragrant scents from fields, vineyards, and gardens, now in the full leafage of June.]

DUMB SHOW
All the English forces converge forward—that is, eastwardly—the centre over the ridges, the right through the Pass to the south, the left down the Bilbao road on the north-west, the bands of the divers regiments striking up the same quick march, "The Downfall of Paris."

SPIRIT OF THE YEARS
You see the scene. And yet you see it not.
What do you notice now?

There immediately is shown visually the electric state of mind that animates WELLINGTON, GRAHAM, HILL, KEMPT, PICTON, COLVILLE, and other responsible ones on the British side; and on the French KING JOSEPH stationary on the hill overlooking his own centre, and surrounded by a numerous staff that includes his adviser MARSHAL JOURDAN, with, far away in the field, GAZAN, D'ERLON, REILLE, and other marshals. This vision, resembling as a whole the interior of a beating brain lit by phosphorescence, in an instant fades back to normal. Anon we see the English hussars with their flying pelisses galloping across the Zadorra on one of the Tres-Puentes in the midst of the field, as had been planned, the English lines in the foreground under HILL pushing the enemy up the slopes; and far in the distance, to the left of Vitoria, whiffs of grey smoke followed by low rumbles show that the left of the English army under GRAHAM is pushing on there.

Bridge after bridge of the half-dozen over the Zadorra is crossed by the British; and WELLINGTON, in the centre with PICTON, seeing the hill and village of Arinez in front of him [eastward] to be weakly held, carries the regiments of the seventh and third divisions in a quick run towards it. Supported by the hussars, they ultimately fight their way to the top, in a chaos of smoke, flame, and booming echoes, loud-voiced PICTON, in an old blue coat and round hat, swearing as he goes.

Meanwhile the French who are opposed to the English right, in the foreground, have been turned by HILL; the heights are all abandoned, and the columns fall back in a confused throng by the road to Vitoria, hard pressed by the British, who capture abandoned guns amid indescribable tumult, till the French make a stand in front of the town.

SPIRIT OF THE PITIES
What's toward in the distance?—say!

SEMICHORUS I OF RUMOURS [aerial music]
Fitfully flash strange sights there; yea,
Unwonted spectacles of sweat and scare
Behind the French, that make a stand
With eighty cannon, match in hand.—
Upon the highway from the town to rear
An eddy of distraction reigns,
Where lumbering treasure, baggage-trains,
Padding pedestrians, haze the atmosphere.

SEMICHORUS II
Men, women, and their children fly,
And when the English over-high
Direct their death-bolts, on this billowy throng
Alight the too far-ranging balls,
Wringing out piteous shrieks and calls
From the pale mob, in monotones loud and long.

SEMICHORUS I
To leftward of the distant din
Reille meantime has been driven in
By Graham's measure overmastering might.—
Henceforward, masses of the foe
Withdraw, and, firing as they go,
Pass rightwise from the cockpit out of sight.

CHORUS
The sunset slants an ochreous shine
Upon the English knapsacked line,
Whose glistering bayonets incline
As bends the hot pursuit across the plain;
And tardily behind them goes
Too many a mournful load of those
Found wound-weak; while with stealthy crawl,
As silence wraps the rear of all,
Cloaked creatures of the starlight strip the slain.

SCENE III

THE SAME. THE ROAD FROM THE TOWN

[With the going down of the sun the English army finds itself in complete possession of the mass of waggons and carriages distantly beheld from the rear—laden with pictures, treasure, flour, vegetables, furniture, finery, parrots, monkeys, and women—most of the male sojourners in the town having taken to their heels and disappeared across the fields.

The road is choked with these vehicles, the women they carry including wives, mistresses, actresses, dancers, nuns, and prostitutes, which struggle through droves of oxen, sheep, goats, horses, asses, and mules— a Noah's-ark of living creatures in one vast procession.

There enters rapidly in front of this throng a carriage containing KING JOSEPH BONAPARTE and an attendant, followed by another vehicle with luggage.]

JOSEPH [inside carriage]
The bare unblinking truth hereon is this:
The Englishry are a pursuing army,
And we a flying brothel! See our men—
They leave their guns to save their mistresses!

[The carriage is fired upon from outside the scene. The KING leaps from the vehicle and mounts a horse.

Enter at full gallop from the left CAPTAIN WYNDHAM and a detachment of the Tenth Hussars in chase of the King's carriage; and from the right a troop of French dragoons, who engage with the hussars and hinder pursuit. Exit KING JOSEPH on horseback; afterwards the hussars and dragoons go out fighting.

The British infantry enter irregularly, led by a sergeant of the Eighty-seventh, mockingly carrying MARSHAL JOURDAN'S baton. The crowd recedes. The soldiers ransack the King's carriages, cut from their frames canvases by Murillo, Velasquez, and Zurbaran, and use them as package-wrappers, throwing the papers and archives into the road.

They next go to a waggon in the background, which contains a large chest. Some of the soldiers burst it with a crash. It is full of money, which rolls into the road. The soldiers begin scrambling, but are restored to order; and they march on.

Enter more companies of infantry, out of control of their officers, who are running behind. They see the dollars, and take up the scramble for them; next ransacking other waggons and abstracting therefrom uniforms, ladies raiment, jewels, plate, wines, and spirits.

Some array them in the finery, and one soldier puts on a diamond necklace; others load themselves with the money still lying about the road. It begins to rain, and a private who has lost his kit cuts a hole in the middle of a deframed old master, and, putting it over his head, wears it as a poncho.

Enter WELLINGTON and others, grimy and perspiring.]

FIRST OFFICER
The men are plundering in all directions!

WELLINGTON
Let 'em. They've striven long and gallantly.
—What documents do I see lying there?

SECOND OFFICER [examining]
The archives of King Joseph's court, my lord;
His correspondence, too, with Bonaparte.

WELLINGTON
We must examine it. It may have use.

[Another company of soldiers enters, dragging some equipages that have lost their horses by the traces being cut. The carriages contain ladies, who shriek and weep at finding themselves captives.]

What women bring they there?

THIRD OFFICER
Mixed sorts, my lord.
The wives of many young French officers,
The mistresses of more—in male attire.
Yon elegant hussar is one, to wit;
She so disguised is of a Spanish house,—
One of the general's loves.

WELLINGTON
Well, pack them off
To-morrow to Pamplona, as you can;
We've neither list nor leisure for their charms.
By God, I never saw so many wh—s
In all my life before!

[Exeunt WELLINGTON, officers, and infantry. A soldier enters with his arm round a lady in rich costume.]

SOLDIER
We must be married, my dear.

LADY [not knowing his language]
Anything, sir, if you'll spare my life!

SOLDIER
There's neither parson nor clerk here. But that don't matter—hey?

LADY
Anything, sir, if you'll spare my life!

SOLDIER
And if we've got to unmarry at cockcrow, why, so be it—hey?

LADY
Anything, sir, if you'll spare my life!

SOLDIER
A sensible 'ooman, whatever it is she says; that I can see by her
pretty face. Come along then, my dear. There'll be no bones broke,
and we'll take our lot with Christian resignation.

[Exeunt soldier and lady. The crowd thins away as darkness closes in, and the growling of artillery ceases, though the wheels of the flying enemy are still heard in the distance. The fires kindled by the soldiers as they make their bivouacs blaze up in the gloom, and throw their glares a long way, revealing on the slopes of the hills many suffering ones who have not yet been carried in. The last victorious regiment comes up from the rear, fifing and drumming ere it reaches its resting-place the last bars of "The Downfall of Paris":—

SCENE IV

A FETE AT VAUXHALL

[It is the Vitoria festival at Vauxhall. The orchestra of the renowned gardens exhibits a blaze of lamps and candles arranged in the shape of a temple, a great artificial sun glowing at the top, and under it in illuminated characters the words "Vitoria" and "Wellington." The band is playing the new air "The Plains of Vitoria."

All round the colonnade of the rotunda are to be read in the illumination the names of Peninsular victories, underneath them figuring the names of British and Spanish generals who led at those battles, surmounted by wreaths of laurel The avenues stretching away from the rotunda into the gardens charm the eyes with their mild multitudinous lights, while festoons of lamps hang from the trees elsewhere, and transparencies representing scenes from the war.

The gardens and saloons are crowded, among those present being the KING'S sons—the DUKES OF YORK, CLARENCE, KENT, and CAMBRIDGE—Ambassadors, peers, and peeresses, and other persons of quality, English and foreign.

In the immediate foreground on the left hand is an alcove, the interior of which is in comparative obscurity. Two foreign attaches enter it and sit down.]

FIRST ATTACHE
Ah—now for the fireworks. They are under the direction of Colonel Congreve.

[At the end of an alley, purposely kept dark, fireworks are discharged.]

SECOND ATTACHE
Very good: very good.—This looks like the Duke of Sussex coming in, I think. Who the lady is with him I don't know.

[Enter the DUKE OF SUSSEX in a Highland dress, attended by several officers in like attire. He walks about the gardens with LADY CHARLOTTE CAMPBELL.]

FIRST ATTACHE
People have been paying a mighty price for tickets—as much as fifteen guineas has been offered, I hear. I had to walk up to the gates; the number of coaches struggling outside prevented my driving near. It was as bad as the battle of Vitoria itself.

SECOND ATTACHE
So Wellington is made Field-Marshal for his achievement.

FIRST ATTACHE
Yes. By the by, you have heard of the effect of the battle upon the Conference at Reichenbach?—that Austria is to join Russia and Prussia against France? So much for Napoleon's marriage! I wonder what he thinks of his respected father-in-law now.

SECOND ATTACHE
Of course, an enormous subsidy is paid to Francis by Great Britain for this face-about?

FIRST ATTACHE
Yes. As Bonaparte says, English guineas are at the bottom of everything!—Ah, here comes Caroline.

[The PRINCESS OF WALES arrives, attended by LADY ANNE HAMILTON and LADY GLENBERVIE. She is conducted forward by the DUKE OF GLOUCESTER and COLONEL ST. LEDGER, and wears a white satin train with a dark embroidered bodice, and a green wreath with diamonds.

Repeated hurrahs greet her from the crowd. She bows courteously.]

SECOND ATTACHE
The people are staunch for her still!... You heard, sir, what Austrian Francis said when he learnt of Vitoria?—"A warm climate seems to agree with my son-in-law no better than a cold one."

FIRST ATTACHE
Ha-ha-ha!
Marvellous it is how this loud victory
Has couched the late blind Europe's Cabinets.
Would I could spell precisely what was phrased
'Twixt Bonaparte and Metternich at Dresden—
Their final word, I ween, till God knows when!—

SECOND ATTACHE
I own to feeling it a sorry thing
That Francis should take English money down
To throw off Bonaparte. 'Tis sordid, mean!
He is his daughter's husband after all.

FIRST ATTACHE
Ay; yes!... They say she knows not of it yet.

SECOND ATTACHE
Poor thing, I daresay it will harry her
When all's revealed. But the inside o't is,
Since Castlereagh's return to power last year
Vienna, like Berlin and Petersburg,
Has harboured England's secret emissaries,

Primed, purse in hand, with the most lavish sums
To knit the league to drag Napoleon down....
[More fireworks.] That's grand.—Here comes one Royal item more.

[The DUCHESS OF YORK enters, attended by her ladies and by the HON. B. CRAVEN and COLONEL BARCLAY. She is received with signals of respect.]

FIRST ATTACHE
She calls not favour forth as Caroline can!

SECOND ATTACHE
To end my words:—Though happy for this realm,
Austria's desertion frankly is, by God,
Rank treachery!

FIRST ATTACHE
Whatever it is, it means
Two hundred thousand swords for the Allies,
And enemies in batches for Napoleon
Leaping from unknown lairs.—Yes, something tells me
That this is the beginning of the end
For Emperor Bonaparte!

[The PRINCESS OF WALES prepares to leave. An English diplomatist joins the attaches in the alcove. The PRINCESS and her ladies go out.]

DIPLOMATIST
I saw you over here, and I came round. Cursed hot and crowded, isn't it?

SECOND ATTACHE
What is the Princess leaving so soon for?

DIPLOMATIST
Oh, she has not been received in the Royal box by the other members of the Royal Family, and it has offended her, though she was told beforehand that she could not be. Poor devil! Nobody invited her here. She came unasked, and she has gone unserved.

FIRST ATTACHE
We shall have to go unserved likewise, I fancy. The scramble at the buffets is terrible.

DIPLOMATIST
And the road from here to Marsh Gate is impassable. Some ladies have been sitting in their coaches for hours outside the hedge there. We shall not get home till noon to-morrow.

A VOICE [from the back]
Take care of your watches! Pickpockets!

FIRST ATTACHE

Good. That relieves the monotony a little.

[Excitement in the throng. When it has subsided the band strikes up a country dance, and stewards with white ribbons and laurel leaves are seen bustling about.]

SECOND ATTACHE
Let us go and look at the dancing. It is "Voulez-vous danser"—no, it is not,—it is "Enrico"—two ladies between two gentlemen.

[They go from the alcove.]

SPIRIT OF THE YEARS
From this phantasmagoria let us roam
To the chief wheel and capstan of the show,
Distant afar. I pray you closely read
What I reveal—wherein each feature bulks
In measure with its value humanly.

[The beholder finds himself, as it were, caught up on high, and while the Vauxhall scene still dimly twinkles below, he gazes southward towards Central Europe—the contorted and attenuated ecorche of the Continent appearing as in an earlier scene, but now obscure under the summer stars.]

Three cities loom out large: Vienna there,
Dresden, which holds Napoleon, over here,
And Leipzig, whither we shall shortly wing,
Out yonderwards. 'Twixt Dresden and Vienna
What thing do you discern?

SPIRIT OF THE PITIES
Something broad-faced,
Flat-folded, parchment-pale, and in its shape
Rectangular; but moving like a cloud
The Dresden way.

SPIRIT OF THE YEARS
Yet gaze more closely on it.

SPIRIT OF THE PITIES
The object takes a letter's lineaments
Though swollen to mainsail measure,—magically,
I gather from your words; and on its face
Are three vast seals, red—signifying blood
Must I suppose? It moves on Dresden town,
And dwarfs the city as it passes by.—
You say Napoleon's there?

SPIRIT OF THE YEARS
The document,

Sized to its big importance, as I told,
Bears in it formal declaration, signed,
Of war by Francis with his late-linked son,
The Emperor of France. Now let us go
To Leipzig city, and await the blow.

[A chaotic gloom ensues, accompanied by a rushing like that of a mighty wind.]

ACT THIRD

SCENE I

LEIPZIG. NAPOLEON'S QUARTERS IN THE REUDNITZ SUBURB

[The sitting-room of a private mansion. Evening. A large stove-fire and candles burning. The October wind is heard without, and the leaded panes of the old windows shake mournfully.]

SEMICHORUS I OF IRONIC SPIRITS [aerial music]
We come; and learn as Time's disordered dear sands run
That Castlereagh's diplomacy has wiled, waxed, won.
The beacons flash the fevered news to eyes keen bent
That Austria's formal words of war are shaped, sealed, sent.

SEMICHORUS II
So; Poland's three despoilers primed by Bull's gross pay
To stem Napoleon's might, he waits the weird dark day;
His proffered peace declined with scorn, in fell force then
They front him, with yet ten-score thousand more massed men.

[At the back of the room CAULAINCOURT, DUKE OF VICENZA, and JOUANNE, one of Napoleon's confidential secretaries, are unpacking and laying out the Emperor's maps and papers. In the foreground BERTHIER, MURAT, LAURISTON, and several officers of Napoleon's suite, are holding a desultory conversation while they await his entry. Their countenances are overcast.]

MURAT
At least, the scheme of marching on Berlin
Is now abandoned.

LAURISTON
Not without high words:
He yielded and gave order prompt for Leipzig
But coldness and reserve have marked his mood
Towards us ever since.

BERTHIER

The march hereto
He has looked on as a retrogressive one,
And that, he ever holds, is courting woe.
To counsel it was doubtless full of risk,
And heaped us with responsibilities;
—Yet 'twas your missive, sire, that settled it [to MURAT].
How stirred he was! "To Leipzig, or Berlin?"
He kept repeating, as he drew and drew
Fantastic figures on the foolscap sheet,—
"The one spells ruin—t'other spells success,
And which is which?"

MURAT [stiffly]
What better could I do?
So far were the Allies from sheering off
As he supposed, that they had moved in march
Full fanfare hither! I was duty-bound
To let him know.

LAURISTON
Assuming victory here,
If he should let the advantage slip him by
As on the Dresden day, he wrecks us all!
'Twas damnable—to ride back from the fight
Inside a coach, as though we had not won!

CAULAINCOURT [from the back]
The Emperor was ill: I have ground for knowing.

[NAPOLEON enters.]

NAPOLEON [buoyantly]
Comrades, the outlook promises us well!

MURAT [dryly]
Right glad are we you tongue such tidings, sire.
To us the stars have visaged differently;
To wit: we muster outside Leipzig here
Levies one hundred and ninety thousand strong.
The enemy has mustered, OUTSIDE US,
Three hundred and fifty thousand—if not more.

NAPOLEON
All that is needful is to conquer them!
We are concentred here: they lie a-spread,
Which shrinks them to two-hundred-thousand power:—
Though that the urgency of victory
Is absolute, I admit.

MURAT
Yea; otherwise
The issue will be worse than Moscow, sire!

[MARMONT, DUKE OF RAGUSA [Wellington's adversary in Spain], is announced, and enters.]

NAPOLEON
Ah, Marmont; bring you in particulars?

MARMONT
Some sappers I have taken captive, sire,
Say the Allies will be at stroke with us
The morning next to to-morrow's.—I am come,
Now, from the steeple-top of Liebenthal,
Where I beheld the enemy's fires bespot
The horizon round with raging eyes of flame:—
My vanward posts, too, have been driven in,
And I need succours—thrice ten thousand, say.

NAPOLEON [coldly]
The enemy vexes not your vanward posts;
You are mistaken.—Now, however, go;
Cross Leipzig, and remain as the reserve.—
Well, gentlemen, my hope herein is this:
The first day to annihilate Schwarzenberg,
The second Blucher. So shall we slip the toils
They are all madding to enmesh us in.

BERTHIER
Few are our infantry to fence with theirs!

NAPOLEON [cheerfully]
We'll range them in two lines instead of three,
And so we shall look stronger by one-third.

BERTHIER [incredulously]
Can they be thus deceived, sire?

NAPOLEON
Can they? Yes!
With all my practice I can err in numbers
At least one-quarter; why not they one-third?
Anyhow, 'tis worth trying at a pinch....

[AUGEREAU is suddenly announced.]

Good! I've not seen him yet since he arrived.

[Enter AUGEREAU.

Here you are then at last, old Augereau!
You have been looked for long.—But you are no more
The Augereau of Castiglione days!

AUGEREAU
Nay, sire! I still should be the Augereau
Of glorious Castiglione, could you give
The boys of Italy back again to me!

NAPOLEON
Well, let it drop.... Only I notice round me
An atmosphere of scopeless apathy
Wherein I do not share.

AUGEREAU
There are reasons, sire,
Good reasons for despondence! As I came
I learnt, past question, that Bavaria
Swerves on the very pivot of desertion.
This adds some threescore thousand to our foes.

NAPOLEON [irritated]
That consummation long has threatened us!...
Would that you showed the steeled fidelity
You used to show! Except me, all are slack!
[To Murat] Why, even you yourself, my brother-in-law,
Have been inclining to abandon me!

MURAT [vehemently]
I, sire? It is not so. I stand and swear
The grievous imputation is untrue.
You should know better than believe these things,
And well remember I have enemies
Who ever wait to slander me to you!

NAPOLEON [more calmly]
Ah yes, yes. That is so.—And yet—and yet
You have deigned to weigh the feasibility
Of treating me as Austria has done!...
But I forgive you. You are a worthy man;
You feel real friendship for me. You are brave.
Yet I was wrong to make a king of you.
If I had been content to draw the line
At vice-king, as with young Eugene, no more,
As he has laboured you'd have laboured, too!

But as full monarch, you have foraged rather
For your own pot than mine!

[MURAT and the marshal are silent, and look at each other with troubled countenances. NAPOLEON goes to the table at the back, and bends over the charts with CAULAINCOURT, dictating desultory notes to the secretaries.]

SPIRIT IRONIC
A seer might say
This savours of a sad Last-Supper talk
'Twixt his disciples and this Christ of war!

[Enter an attendant.]

ATTENDANT
The Saxon King and Queen and the Princess
Enter the city gates, your Majesty.
They seek the shelter of the civic walls
Against the risk of capture by Allies.

NAPOLEON
Ah, so? My friend Augustus, is he near?
I will be prompt to meet him when he comes,
And safely quarter him. [He returns to the map.]

[An interval. The clock strikes midnight. The EMPEROR rises abruptly, sighs, and comes forward.]

I now retire,
Comrades. Good-night, good-night. Remember well
All must prepare to grip with gory death
In the now voidless battle. It will be
A great one and a critical; one, in brief,
That will seal France's fate, and yours, and mine!

ALL [fervidly]
We'll do our utmost, by the Holy Heaven!

NAPOLEON
Ah—what was that? [He pulls back the window-curtain.]

SEVERAL
It is our enemies,
Whose southern hosts are signalling to their north.

[A white rocket is beheld high in the air. It is followed by a second, and a third. There is a pause, during which NAPOLEON and the rest wait motionless. In a minute or two, from the opposite side of the city, three coloured rockets are sent up, in evident answer to the three white ones. NAPOLEON muses, and lets the curtain drop.]

NAPOLEON
Yes, Schwarzenberg to Blucher.... It must be
To show that they are ready. So are we!

[He goes out without saying more. The marshals and other officers withdraw. The room darkens and ends the scene.]

SCENE II

THE SAME. THE CITY AND THE BATTLEFIELD

[Leipzig is viewed in aerial perspective from a position above the south suburbs, and reveals itself as standing in a plain, with rivers and marshes on the west, north, and south of it, and higher ground to the east and south-east.

At this date it is somewhat in she shape of the letter D, the straight part of which is the river Pleisse. Except as to this side it is surrounded by armies—the inner horseshoe of them being the French defending the city; the outer horseshoe being the Allies about to attack it.

Far over the city—as it were at the top of the D—at Lindenthal, we see MARMONT stationed to meet BLUCHER when he arrives on that side. To the right of him is NEY, and further off to the right, on heights eastward, MACDONALD. Then round the curve towards the south in order, AUGEREAU, LAURISTON [behind whom is NAPOLEON himself and the reserve of Guards], VICTOR [at Wachau], and PONIATOWSKI, near the Pleisse River at the bottom of the D. Near him are the cavalry of KELLERMANN and MILHAUD, and in the same direction MURAT with his, covering the great avenues of approach on the south.

Outside all these stands SCHWARZENBERG'S army, of which, opposed to MACDONALD and LAURISTON, are KLEINAU'S Austrians and ZIETEN'S Prussians, covered on the flank by Cossacks under PLATOFF. Opposed to VICTOR and PONIATOWSKI are MEERFELDT and Hesse-Homburg's Austrians, WITTGENSTEIN'S Russians, KLEIST'S Prussians, GUILAY'S Austrians, with LICHTENSTEIN'S and THIELMANN'S light troops: thus reaching round across the Elster into the morass on our near left—the lower point of the D.]

SEMICHORUS I OF RUMOURS [aerial music]
This is the combat of Napoleon's hope,
But not of his assurance! Shrunk in power
He broods beneath October's clammy cope,
While hemming hordes wax denser every hour.

SEMICHORUS II
He knows, he knows that though in equal fight
He stand s heretofore the matched of none,
A feeble skill is propped by numbers' might,
And now three hosts close round to crush out one!

DUMB SHOW

The Leipzig clocks imperturbably strike nine, and the battle which is to decide the fate of Europe, and perhaps the world, begins with three booms from the line of the allies. They are the signal for a general cannonade of devastating intensity.

So massive is the contest that we soon fail to individualize the combatants as beings, and can only observe them as amorphous drifts, clouds, and waves of conscious atoms, surging and rolling together; can only particularize them by race, tribe, and language. Nationalities from the uttermost parts of Asia here meet those from the Atlantic edge of Europe for the first and last time. By noon the sound becomes a loud droning, uninterrupted and breve-like, as from the pedal of an organ kept continuously down.

CHORUS OF RUMOURS
Now triple battle beats about the town,
And now contracts the huge elastic ring
Of fighting flesh, as those within go down,
Or spreads, as those without show faltering!

It becomes apparent that the French have a particular intention, the Allies only a general one. That of the French is to break through the enemy's centre and surround his right. To this end NAPOLEON launches fresh columns, and simultaneously OUDINOT supports VICTOR against EUGENE OF WURTEMBERG'S right, while on the other side of him the cavalry of MILHAUD and KELLERMAN prepares to charge.

NAPOLEON'S combination is successful, and drives back EUGENE. Meanwhile SCHWARZENBERG is stuck fast, useless in the marshes between the Pleisse and the Elster.

By three o'clock the Allied centre, which has held out against the assaults of the French right and left, is broken through by cavalry under MURAT, LATOUR-MAUBOURG, and KELLERMANN.

The bells of Leipzig ring.

CHORUS OF THE PITIES
Those chimings, ill-advised and premature!
Who knows if such vast valour will endure?

The Austro-Russians are withdrawn from the marshes by SCHWARZENBERG. But the French cavalry also get entangled in the swamps, and simultaneously MARMONT is beaten at Mockern.

Meanwhile NEY, to the north of Leipzig, having heard the battle raging southward, leaves his position to assist it. He has nearly arrived when he hears BLUCHER attacking at the point he came from, and sends back some of his divisions.

BERTRAND has kept open the west road to Lindenau and the Rhine, the only French line of retreat.

Evening finds the battle a drawn one. With the nightfall three blank shots reverberate hollowly.

SEMICHORUS I OF RUMOURS
They sound to say that, for this moaning night,
As Nature sleeps, so too shall sleep the fight;
Neither the victor.

SEMICHORUS II
But, for France and him,
Half-won is losing!

CHORUS
Yea, his hopes drop dim,
Since nothing less than victory to-day
Had saved a cause whose ruin is delay!
The night gets thicker and no more is seen.

SCENE III

THE SAME, FROM THE TOWER OF THE PLEISSENBURG

[The tower commands a view of a great part of the battlefield. Day has just dawned, and citizens, saucer-eyed from anxiety and sleeplessness, are discover watching.]

FIRST CITIZEN
The wind increased at midnight while I watched,
With flapping showers, and clouds that combed the moon,
Till dawn began outheaving this huge day,
Pallidly—as if scared by its own issue;
This day that the Allies with bonded might
Have vowed to deal their felling finite blow.

SECOND CITIZEN
So must it be! They have welded close the coop
Wherein our luckless Frenchmen are enjailed
With such compression that their front has shrunk
From five miles' farness to but half as far.—
Men say Napoleon made resolve last night
To marshal a retreat. If so, his way
Is by the Bridge of Lindenau.

[They look across in the cold east light at the long straight causeway from the Ranstadt Gate at the north-west corner of the town, and the Lindenau bridge over the Elster beyond.]

FIRST CITIZEN
Last night I saw, like wolf-packs, hosts appear
Upon the Dresden road; and then, anon,
The already stout arrays of Schwarzenberg

Grew stoutened more. I witnessed clearly, too,
Just before dark, the bands of Bernadotte
Come, hemming in the north more thoroughly.
The horizon glowered with a thousand fires
As the unyielding circle shut around.

[As it grows light they scan and define the armies.]

THIRD CITIZEN
Those lying there, 'twixt Connewitz and Dolitz,
Are the right wing of horse Murat commands.
Next, Poniatowski, Victor, and the rest.
Out here, Napoleon's centre at Probstheida,
Where he has bivouacked. Those round this way
Are his left wing with Ney, that face the north
Between Paunsdorf and Gohlis.—Thus, you see
They are skilfully sconced within the villages,
With cannon ranged in front. And every copse,
Dingle, and grove is packed with riflemen.

[The heavy sky begins to clear with the full arrival of the morning. The sun bursts out, and the
previously dark and gloomy masses glitter in the rays. It is now seven o'clock, and with the shining of
the sun, the battle is resumed.

The army of Bohemia to the south and east, in three great columns, marches concentrically upon
NAPOLEON'S new and much-contracted line —the first column of thirty-five thousand under
BENNIGSEN; the second, the central, forty-five thousand under BARCLAY DE TOLLY; the third, twenty-
five thousand under the PRINCE OF HESSE-HOMBURG.

An interval of suspense.]

FIRST CITIZEN
Ah, see! The French bend, falter, and fall back.

[Another interval. Then a huge rumble of artillery resounds from the north.]

SEMICHORUS OF RUMOURS [aerial music]
Now Blucher has arrived; and now falls to!
Marmont withdraws before him. Bernadotte
Touching Bennigsen, joins attack with him,
And Ney must needs recede. This serves as sign
To Schwarzenberg to bear upon Probstheida—
Napoleon's keystone and dependence here.
But for long whiles he fails to win his will,
The chief being nigh—outmatching might with skill.

SEMICHORUS II
Ney meanwhile, stung still sharplier, still withdraws

Nearer the town, and met by new mischance,
Finds him forsaken by his Saxon wing—
Fair files of thrice twelve thousand footmanry.
But rallying those still true with signs and calls,
He warely closes up his remnant to the walls.

SEMICHORUS I
Around Probstheida still the conflict rolls
Under Napoleon's eye surpassingly.
Like sedge before the scythe the sections fall
And bayonets slant and reek. Each cannon-blaze
Makes the air thick with human limbs; while keen
Contests rage hand to hand. Throats shout "advance,"
And forms walm, wallow, and slack suddenly.
Hot ordnance split and shiver and rebound,
And firelocks fouled and flintless overstrew the ground.

SEMICHORUS II
At length the Allies, daring tumultuously,
Find them inside Probstheida. There is fixed
Napoleon's cardinal and centre hold.
But need to loose it grows his gloomy fear
As night begins to brown and treacherous mists appear.

CHORUS
Then, on the three fronts of this reaching field,
A furious, far, and final cannonade
Burns from two thousand mouths and shakes the plain,
And hastens the sure end! Towards the west
Bertrand keeps open the retreating-way,
Along which wambling waggons since the noon
Have crept in closening file. Dusk draws around;
The marching remnants drowse amid their talk,
And worn and harrowed horses slumber as the walk.

[In the darkness of the distance spread cries from the maimed animals and the wounded men.
Multitudes of the latter contrive to crawl into the city, until the streets are full of them. Their voices are
heard calling.]

SECOND CITIZEN
They cry for water! Let us go down,
And do what mercy may.

[Exeunt citizens from the tower.]

SPIRIT OF THE PITIES
A fire is lit
Near to the Thonberg wind-wheel. Can it be

Napoleon tarries yet? Let us go see.

[The distant firelight becomes clearer and closer.]

SCENE IV

THE SAME. AT THE THONBERG WINDMILL

[By the newly lighted fire NAPOLEON is seen walking up and down, much agitated and worn. With him
are MURAT, BERTHIER, AUGEREAU, VICTOR, and other marshals of corps that have been engaged in this
part of the field—all perspiring, muddy, and fatigued.]

NAPOLEON
Baseness so gross I had not guessed of them!—
The thirty thousand false Bavarians
I looked on losing not unplacidly;
But these troth-swearing sober Saxonry
I reckoned staunch by virtue of their king!
Thirty-five thousand and gone! It magnifies
A failure into a catastrophe....
Murat, we must retreat precipitately,
And not as hope had dreamed! Begin it then
This very hour.—Berthier, write out the orders.—
Let me sit down.

[A chair is brought out from the mill. NAPOLEON sinks into it, and BERTHIER, stooping over the fire,
begins writing to the Emperor's dictation, the marshals looking with gloomy faces at the flaming logs.

NAPOLEON has hardly dictated a line when he stops short. BERTHIER turns round and finds that he has
dropt asleep.]

MURAT [sullenly]
Far better not disturb him;
He'll soon enough awake!

[They wait, muttering to one another in tones expressing weary indifference to issues. NAPOLEON
sleeps heavily for a quarter of and hour, during which the moon rises over the field. At the end he starts
up stares around him with astonishment.]

NAPOLEON
Am I awake?
Or is this all a dream?—Ah, no. Too real!...
And yet I have seen ere now a time like this.

[The dictation is resumed. While it is in progress there can be heard between the words of NAPOLEON
the persistent cries from the plain, rising and falling like those of a vast rookery far away, intermingled

with the trampling of hoofs and the rumble of wheels. The bivouac fires of the engirdling enemy glow all around except for a small segment to the west—the track of retreat, still kept open by BERTRAND, and already taken by the baggage-waggons.

The orders for its adoption by the entire army being completed, NAPOLEON bids adieu to his marshals, and rides with BERTHIER and CAULAINCOURT into Leipzig. Exeunt also the others.]

SEMICHORUS I OF THE PITIES
Now, as in the dream of one sick to death,
There comes a narrowing room
That pens him, body and limbs and breath,
To wait a hideous doom,

SEMICHORUS II
So to Napoleon in the hush
That holds the town and towers
Through this dire night, a creeping crush
Seems inborne with the hours.

[The scene closes under a rimy mist, which makes a lurid cloud of the firelights.]

SCENE V

THE SAME. A STREET NEAR THE RANSTADT GATE

[High old-fashioned houses form the street, along which, from the east of the city, is streaming a confusion of waggons, in hurried exit through the gate westward upon the highroad to Lindenau, Lutzen, and the Rhine.

In front of an inn called the "Prussian Arms" are some attendants of NAPOLEON waiting with horses.]

FIRST OFFICER
He has just come from bidding the king and queen
A long good-bye.... Is it that they will pay
For his indulgence of their past ambition
By sharing now his ruin? Much the king
Did beg him to leave them to their lot,
And shun the shame of capture needlessly.
[He looks anxiously towards the door.]
I would he'd haste! Each minute is of price.

SECOND OFFICER
The king will come to terms with the Allies.
They will not hurt him. Though he has lost his all,
His case is not like ours!

[The cheers of the approaching enemy grow louder. NAPOLEON comes out from the "Prussian Arms," haggard and in disordered attire. He is about to mount, but, perceiving the blocked state of the street, he hesitates.]

NAPOLEON
God, what a crowd!
I shall more quickly gain the gate afoot.
There is a byway somewhere, I suppose?

[A citizen approaches out of the inn.]

CITIZEN
This alley, sire, will speed you to the gate;
I shall be honoured much to point the way.

NAPOLEON
Then do, good friend. [To attendants] Bring on the horses there;
I if arrive soonest I will wait for you.

[The citizen shows NAPOLEON the way into the alley.]

CITIZEN
A garden's at the end, your Majesty,
Through which you pass. Beyond there is a door
That opens to the Elster bank unbalked.

[NAPOLEON disappears into the alley. His attendants plunge amid the traffic with the horses, and thread their way down the street.

Another citizen comes from the door of the inn and greets the first.]

FIRST CITIZEN
He's gone!

SECOND CITIZEN
I'll see if he succeed.

[He re-enters the inn and soon appears at an upper window.]

FIRST CITIZEN [from below]
You see him?

SECOND CITIZEN [gazing]
He is already at the garden-end;
Now he has passed out to the river-brim,
And plods along it toward the Ranstadt Gate....
He finds no horses for him!... And the crowd
Thrusts him about, none recognizing him.

Ah—now the horses do arrive. He mounts,
And hurries through the arch.... Again I see him—
Now he's upon the causeway in the marsh;
Now rides across the bridge of Lindenau...
And now, among the troops that choke the road
I lose all sight of him.

[A third citizen enters from the direction NAPOLEON has taken.]

THIRD CITIZEN [breathlessly]
I have seen him go!
And while he passed the gate I stood i' the crowd
So close I could have touched him! Few discerned
In one so soiled the erst Arch-Emperor!—
In the lax mood of him who has lost all
He stood inert there, idly singing thin:
"Malbrough s'en va-t-en guerre!"—until his suite
Came up with horses.

SECOND CITIZEN [still gazing afar]
Poniatowski's Poles
Wearily walk the level causeway now;
Also, meseems, Macdonald's corps and Reynier's.
The frail-framed, new-built bridge has broken down:
They've but the old to cross by.

FIRST CITIZEN
Feeble foresight!
They should have had a dozen.

SECOND CITIZEN
All the corps—
Macdonald's, Poniatowski's, Reynier's—all—
Confusedly block the entrance to the bridge.
And—verily Blucher's troops are through the town,
And are debouching from the Ranstadt Gate
Upon the Frenchmen's rear!

[A thunderous report stops his words, echoing through the city from the direction in which he is gazing, and rattling all the windows. A hoarse chorus of cries becomes audible immediately after.]

FIRST, THIRD, ETC., CITIZENS
Ach, Heaven!—what's that?

SECOND CITIZEN
The bridge of Lindenau has been upblown!

SEMICHORUS I OF THE PITIES [aerial music]

There leaps to the sky and earthen wave,
And stones, and men, as though
Some rebel churchyard crew updrave
Their sepulchres from below.

SEMICHORUS II
To Heaven is blown Bridge Lindenau;
Wrecked regiments reel therefrom;
And rank and file in masses plough
The sullen Elster-Strom.

SEMICHORUS I
A gulf is Lindenau; and dead
Are fifties, hundreds, tens;
And every current ripples red
With marshals' blood and men's.

SEMICHORUS II
The smart Macdonald swims therein,
And barely wins the verge;
Bold Poniatowski plunges in
Never to re-emerge!

FIRST CITIZEN
Are not the French across as yet, God save them?

SECOND CITIZEN [still gazing above]
Nor Reynier's corps, Macdonald's, Lauriston's,
Nor yet the Poles.... And Blucher's troops approach,
And all the French this side are prisoners.
—Now for our handling by the Prussian host;
Scant courtesy for our king!

[Other citizens appear beside him at the window, and further conversation continues entirely above.]

CHORUS OF IRONIC SPIRITS
The Battle of the Nations now is closing,
And all is lost to One, to many gained;
The old dynastic routine reimposing,
The new dynastic structure unsustained.

Now every neighbouring realm is France's warder,
And smirking satisfaction will be feigned:
The which is seemlier?—so-called ancient order,
Or that the hot-breath'd war-horse ramp unreined?

[The October night thickens and curtains the scene.]

SCENE VI

THE PYRENEES. NEAR THE RIVER NIVELLE

[Evening. The dining-room of WELLINGTON'S quarters. The table is laid for dinner. The battle of the Nivelle has just been fought.

Enter WELLINGTON, HILL, BERESFORD, STEWART, HOPE, CLINTON, COLBORNE, COLE, KEMPT [with a bound-up wound], and other officers. WELLINGTON

It is strange that they did not hold their grand position more tenaciously against us to-day. By God, I don't quite see why we should have beaten them!

COLBORNE
My impression is that they had the stiffness taken out of them by something they had just heard of. Anyhow, startling news of some kind was received by those of the Eighty-eighth we took in the signal-redoubt after I summoned the Commandant.

WELLINGTON
Oh, what news?

COLBORNE
I cannot say, my lord, I only know that the latest number of the Imperial Gazette was seen in the hands of some of them before the capture. They had been reading the contents, and were cast down.

WELLINGTON
That's interesting. I wonder what the news could have been?

HILL
Something about Boney's army in Saxony would be most probable. Though I question if there's time yet for much to have been decided there.

BERESFORD
Well, I wouldn't say that. A hell of a lot of things may have happened there by this time.

COLBORNE
It was tantalizing, but they were just able to destroy the paper before we could prevent them.

WELLINGTON
Did you question them?

COLBORNE
Oh yes. But they stayed sulking at being taken, and would tell us nothing, pretending that they knew nothing. Whether much were going on, they said, or little, between the army of the Emperor and the army of the Allies, it was none of their business to relate it; so they kept a gloomy silence for the most part.

WELLINGTON
They will cheer up a bit and be more communicative when they have had some dinner.

COLE
They are dining here, my lord?

WELLINGTON
I sent them an invitation an hour ago, which they have accepted.
I could do no less, poor devils. They'll be here in a few minutes.
See that they have plenty of Madeira to whet their whistles with.
It well screw them up into a better key, and they'll not be so reserved.

[The conversation on the day's battle becomes general. Enter as guests French officers of the Eighty-eighth regiment now prisoners on parole. They are welcomed by WELLINGTON and the staff, and all sit down to dinner.

For some time the meal proceeds almost in silence; but wine is passed freely, and both French and English officers become talkative and merry.

WELLINGTON [to the French Commandant]
More cozy this, sir, than—I'll warrant me—
You found it in that damned redoubt to-day?

COMMANDANT
The devil if 'tis not, monseigneur, sure!

WELLINGTON
So 'tis for us who were outside, by God!

COMMANDANT [gloomily]
No; we were not at ease! Alas, my lord,
'Twas more than flesh and blood could do, to fight
After such paralyzing tidings came.
More life may trickle out of men through thought
Than through a gaping wound.

WELLINGTON
Your reference
Bears on the news from Saxony, I infer?

SECOND FRENCH OFFICER
Yes: on the Emperor's ruinous defeat
At Leipzig city—brought to our startled heed
By one of the Gazettes just now arrived.

[All the English officers stop speaking, and listen eagerly.]

WELLINGTON
Where are the Emperor's headquarters now?

COMMANDANT
My lord, there are no headquarters.

WELLINGTON
No headquarters?

COMMANDANT
There are no French headquarters now, my lord,
For there is no French army! France's fame
Is fouled. And how, then, could we fight to-day
With our hearts in our shoes!

WELLINGTON
Why, that bears out
What I but lately said; it was not like
The brave men who have faced and foiled me here
So many a long year past, to give away
A stubborn station quite so readily.

BERESFORD
And what, messieurs, ensued at Leipzig then?

SEVERAL FRENCH OFFICERS
Why, sirs, should we conceal it? Thereupon
Part of our army took the Lutzen road;
Behind a blown-up bridge. Those in advance
Arrived at Lutzen with the Emperor—
The scene of our once famous victory!
In such sad sort retreat was hurried on,
Erfurt was gained with Blucher hot at heel.
To cross the Rhine seemed then our only hope;
Alas, the Austrians and the Bavarians
Faced us in Hanau Forest, led by Wrede,
And dead-blocked our escape.

WELLINGTON
Ha. Did they though?

SECOND FRENCH OFFICER
But if brave hearts were ever desperate,
Sir, we were desperate then! We pierced them through,
Our loss unrecking. So by Frankfurt's walls
We fared to Mainz, and there recrossed the Rhine.
A funeral procession, so we seemed,
Upon the long bridge that had rung so oft

To our victorious feet!... What since has coursed
We know not, gentlemen. But this we know,
That Germany echoes no French footfall!

AN ENGLISH OFFICER
One sees not why it should.

SECOND FRENCH OFFICER
We'll leave it so.

[Conversation on the Leipzig disaster continues till the dinner ends The French prisoners courteously
take their leave and go out.]

WELLINGTON
Very good set of fellows. I could wish
They all were mine!...Well, well; there was no crime
In trying to ascertain these fat events:
They would have sounded soon from other tongues.

HILL
It looks like the first scene of act the last
For our and all men's foe!

WELLINGTON
I count to meet
The Allies upon the cobble-stones of Paris
Before another half-year's suns have shone.
—But there's some work for us to do here yet:
The dawn must find us fording the Nivelle!

[Exeunt WELLINGTON and officers. The room darkens.]

ACT FOURTH

SCENE I

THE UPPER RHINE

[The view is from a vague altitude over the beautiful country traversed by the Upper Rhine, which
stretches through it in birds-eye perspective. At this date in Europe's history the stream forms the
frontier between France and Germany.

It is the morning of New Year's Day, and the shine of the tardy sun reaches the fronts of the beetling
castles, but scarcely descends far enough to touch the wavelets of the river winding leftwards across the
many-leagued picture from Schaffhausen to Coblenz.]

DUMB SHOW

At first nothing—not even the river itself—seems to move in the panorama. But anon certain strange dark patches in the landscape, flexuous and riband-shaped, are discerned to be moving slowly.

Only one movable object on earth is large enough to be conspicuous herefrom, and that is an army. The moving shapes are armies.

The nearest, almost beneath us, is defiling across the river by a bridge of boats, near the junction of the Rhine and the Neckar, where the oval town of Mannheim, standing in the fork between the two rivers, has from here the look of a human head in a cleft stick. Martial music from many bands strikes up as the crossing is effected, and the undulating columns twinkle as if they were scaly serpents.

SPIRIT OF RUMOUR
It is the Russian host, invading France!

Many miles to the left, down-stream, near the little town of Caube, another army is seen to be simultaneously crossing the pale current, its arms and accoutrements twinkling in like manner.

SPIRIT OF RUMOUR
Thither the Prussian levies, too, advance!

Turning now to the right, far away by Basel [beyond which the Swiss mountains close the scene], a still larger train of war-geared humanity, two hundred thousand strong, is discernible. It has already crossed the water, which is much narrower here, and has advanced several miles westward, where its ductile mass of greyness and glitter is beheld parting into six columns, that march on in flexuous courses of varying direction.

SPIRIT OF RUMOUR
There glides carked Austria's invading force!—
Panting, too, Paris-wards with foot and horse,
Of one intention with the other twain,
And Wellington, from the south, in upper Spain.

All these dark and grey columns, converging westward by sure degrees, advance without opposition. They glide on as if by gravitation, in fluid figures, dictated by the conformation of the country, like water from a burst reservoir; mostly snake-shaped, but occasionally with batrachian and saurian outlines. In spite of the immensity of this human mechanism on its surface, the winter landscape wears an impassive look, as if nothing were happening.

Evening closes in, and the Dumb Show is obscured.

SCENE II

PARIS. THE TUILERIES

[It is Sunday just after mass, and the principal officers of the National Guard are assembled in the Salle des Marechaux. They stand in an attitude of suspense, some with the print of sadness on their faces, some with that of perplexity.

The door leading from the Hall to the adjoining chapel is thrown open. There enter from the chapel with the last notes of the service the EMPEROR NAPOLEON and the EMPRESS; and simultaneously from a door opposite MADAME DE MONTESQUIOU, the governess, who carries in her arms the KING OF ROME, now a fair child between two and three. He is clothed in a miniature uniform of the Guards themselves.

MADAM DE MONTESQUIOU brings forward the child and sets him on his feet near his mother. NAPOLEON, with a mournful smile, giving one hand to the boy and the other to MARIE LOUISE, en famille, leads them forward. The Guard bursts into cheers.]

NAPOLEON
Gentlemen of the National Guard and friends,
I have to leave you; and before I fare
To Heaven know what of personal destiny,
I give into your loyal guardianship
Those dearest in the world to me; my wife,
The Empress, and my son the King of Rome.—
I go to shield your roofs and kin from foes
Who have dared to pierce the fences of our land;
And knowing that you house those dears of mine,
I start afar in all tranquillity,
Stayed by my trust in your proved faithfulness.

[Enthusiastic cheers for the Guard.]

OFFICERS [with emotion]
We proudly swear to justify the trust!
And never will we see another sit
Than you, or yours, on the great throne of France.

NAPOLEON
I ratify the Empress' regency,
And re-confirm it on last year's lines,
My bother Joseph stoutening her rule
As the Lieutenant-General of the State.—
Vex her with no divisions; let regard
For property, for order, and for France
Be chief with all. Know, gentlemen, the Allies
Are drunken with success. Their late advantage
They have handled wholly for their own gross gain,
And made a pastime of my agony.

That I go clogged with cares I sadly own;
Yet I go primed with hope; ay, in despite

Of a last sorrow that has sunk upon me,—
The grief of hearing, good and constant friends,
That my own sister's consort, Naples' king,
Blazons himself a backer of the Allies,
And marches with a Neapolitan force
Against our puissance under Prince Eugene.

The varied operations to ensue
May bring the enemy largely Paris-wards;
But suffer no alarm; before long days
I will annihilate by flank and rear
Those who have risen to trample on our soil;
And as I have done so many and proud a time,
Come back to you with ringing victory!—
Now, see: I personally present to you
My son and my successor ere I go.

[He takes the child in his arms and carries him round to the officers severally. They are much affected and raise loud cheers.]

You stand by him and her? You swear as much?

OFFICERS
We do!

NAPOLEON
This you repeat—you promise it?

OFFICERS
We promise. May the dynasty live for ever!

[Their shouts, which spread to the Carrousel without, are echoed by the soldiers of the Guard assembled there. The EMPRESS is now in tears, and the EMPEROR supports her.]

MARIE LOUISE
Such whole enthusiasm I have never known!—
Not even from the Landwehr of Vienna.

[Amid repeated protestations and farewells NAPOLEON, the EMPRESS, the KING OF ROME, MADAME DE MONTESQUIOU, etc. go out in one direction, and the officers of the National Guard in another.

The curtain falls for an interval.

When it rises again the apartment is in darkness, and its atmosphere chilly. The January night-wind howls without. Two servants enter hastily, and light candles and a fire. The hands of the clock are pointing to three.

The room is hardly in order when the EMPEROR enters, equipped for the intended journey; and with him, his left arm being round her waist, walks MARIE LOUISE in a dressing-gown. On his right arm he carries the KING OF ROME, and in his hand a bundle of papers. COUNT BERTRAND and a few members of the household follow.

Reaching the middle of the room, he kisses the child and embraces the EMPRESS, who is tearful, the child weeping likewise. NAPOLEON takes the papers to the fire, thrusts them in, and watches them consume; then burns other bundles brought by his attendants.]

NAPOLEON [gloomily]
Better to treat them thus; since no one knows
What comes, or into whose hands he may fall!

MARIE LOUISE
I have an apprehension-unexplained—
That I shall never see you any more!

NAPOLEON
Dismiss such fears. You may as well as not.
As things are doomed to be they will be, dear.
If shadows must come, let them come as though
The sun were due and you were trusting to it:
'Twill teach the world it wrongs in bringing them.

[They embrace finally. Exeunt NAPOLEON, etc. Afterwards MARIE LOUISE and the child.]

SPIRIT OF THE YEARS
Her instinct forwardly is keen in cast,
And yet how limited. True it may be
They never more will meet; although—to use
The bounded prophecy I am dowered with—
The screen that will maintain their severance
Would pass her own believing; proving it
No gaol-grille, no scath of scorching war,
But this persuasion, pressing on her pulse
To breed aloofness and a mind averse;
Until his image in her soul will shape
Dwarfed as a far Colossus on a plain,
Or figure-head that smalls upon the main.

[The lights are extinguished and the hall is left in darkness.]

SCENE III

THE SAME. THE APARTMENTS OF THE EMPRESS

[A March morning, verging on seven o'clock, throws its cheerless stare into the private drawing-room of MARIE LOUISE, animating the gilt furniture to only a feeble shine. Two chamberlains of the palace are there in waiting. They look from the windows and yawn.]

FIRST CHAMBERLAIN
Here's a watering for spring hopes! Who would have supposed when the Emperor left, and appointed her Regent, that she and the Regency too would have to scurry after in so short a time!

SECOND CHAMBERLAIN
Was a course decided on last night?

FIRST CHAMBERLAIN
Yes. The Privy Council sat till long past midnight, debating the burning question whether she and the child should remain or not. Some were one way, some the other. She settled the matter by saying she would go.

SECOND CHAMBERLAIN
I thought it might come to that. I heard the alarm beating all night to assemble the National Guard; and I am told that some volunteers have marched out to support Marmot. But they are a mere handful: what can they do?

[A clatter of wheels and a champing and prancing of horses is heard outside the palace. MENEVAL enters, and divers officers of the household; then from her bedroom at the other end MARIE LOUISE, in a travelling dress and hat, leading the KING OF ROME, attired for travel likewise. She looks distracted and pale.

Next come the DUCHESS OF MONTEBELLO, lady of honour, the COUNTESS DE MONTESQUIOU, ladies of the palace, and others, all in travelling trim.]

KING OF ROME [plaintively]
Why are we doing these strange things, mamma,
And what did we get up so early for?

MARIE LOUISE
I cannot, dear, explain. So many events
Enlarge and make so many hours of one,
That it would be too hard to tell them now.

KING OF ROME
But you know why we a setting out like this?
Is it because we fear our enemies?

MARIE LOUISE
We are not sure that we are going yet.
I may be needful; but don't ask me here.
Some time I will tell you.

[She sits down irresolutely, and bestows recognitions on the assembled officials with a preoccupied air.]

KING OF ROME [in a murmur]
I like being here best;
And I don't want to go I know not where!

MARIE LOUISE
Run, dear to Mamma 'Quiou and talk to her
[He goes across to MADAME DE MONTESQUIOU.]
I hear that women of the Royalist hope
[To the DUCHESS OF MONTEBELLO]
Have bent them busy in their private rooms
With working white cockades these several days.—
Yes—I must go!

DUCHESS OF MONTEBELLO
But why yet, Empress dear?
We may soon gain good news; some messenger
Hie from the Emperor or King Joseph hither?

MARIE LOUISE
King Joseph I await. He's gone to eye
The outposts, with the Ministers of War,
To learn the scope and nearness of the Allies;
He should almost be back.

[A silence, till approaching feet are suddenly heard outside the door.]

Ah, here he comes;
Now we shall know!

[Enter precipitately not Joseph but officers of the National Guard and others.]

OFFICERS
Long live the Empress-regent!
Do not quit Paris, pray, your Majesty.
Remain, remain. We plight us to defend you!

MARIE LOUISE [agitated]
Gallant messieurs, I thank you heartily.
But by the Emperor's biddance I am bound.
He has vowed he'd liefer see me and my son
Blanched at the bottom of the smothering Seine
Than in the talons of the foes of France.—
To keep us sure from such, then, he ordained
Our swift withdrawal with the Ministers
Towards the Loire, if enemies advanced
In overmastering might. They do advance;
Marshal Marmont and Mortier are repulsed,

And that has come whose hazard he foresaw.
All is arranged; the treasure is awheel,
And papers, seals, and cyphers packed therewith.

OFFICERS [dubiously]
Yet to leave Paris is to court disaster!

MARIE LOUISE [with petulance]
I shall do what I say!... I don't know what—
What SHALL I do!

[She bursts into tears and rushes into her bedroom, followed by the young KING and some of her ladies. There is a painful silence, broken by sobbings and expostulations within. Re-enter one of the ladies.]

LADY
She's sorely overthrown;
She flings herself upon the bed distraught.
She says, "My God, let them make up their minds
To one or other of these harrowing ills,
And force to't, and end my agony!"

[An official enters at the main door.]

OFFICIAL
I am sent here by the Minister of War
To her Imperial Majesty the Empress.

[Re-enter MARIE LOUISE and the KING OF ROME.]

Your Majesty, my mission is to say
Imperious need dictates your instant flight.
A vanward regiment of the Prussian packs
Has gained the shadow of the city walls.

MENEVAL
They are armed Europe's scouts!

[Enter CAMBACERES the Arch-Chancellor, COUNT BEAUHARNAIS, CORVISART the physician, DE BAUSSET, DE CANISY the equerry, and others.]

CAMBACERES
Your Majesty,
There's not a trice to lose. The force well-nigh
Of all compacted Europe crowds on us,
And clamours at the walls!

BEAUHARNAIS
If you stay longer,

You stay to fall into the Cossacks hands.
The people, too, are waxing masterful:
They think the lingering of your Majesty
Makes Paris more a peril for themselves
Than a defence for you. To fight is fruitless,
And wanton waste of life. You have nought to do
But go; and I, and all the Councillors,
Will follow you.

MARIE LOUISE
Then I was right to say
That I would go! Now go I surely will,
And let none try to hinder me again!

[She prepares to leave.]

KING OF ROME [crying]
I will not go! I like to live here best!
Don't go to Rambouillet, mamma; please don't.
It is a nasty place! Let us stay here.
O Mamma 'Quiou, stay with me here; pray stay!

MARIE LOUISE [to the Equerry]
Bring him down.

[Exit MARIE LOUISE in tears, followed by ladies-in-waiting and others.]

DE CANISY
Come now, Monseigneur, come.

[He catches up the boy in his arms and prepares to follow the Empress.]

KING OF ROME [kicking]
No, no, no! I don't want to go away from my house—I don't want to! Now papa is away I am the
master! [He clings to the door as the equerry is bearing him through it.]

DE CANISY
But you must go.

[The child's fingers are pulled away. Exit DE CANISY with the King OF ROME, who is heard screaming as
he is carried down the staircase.]

MADAME DE MONTESQUIOU
I feel the child is right!
A premonition has enlightened him.
She ought to stay. But, ah, the die is cast!

[MADAME DE MONTESQUIOU and the remainder of the party follow, and the room is left empty. Enter servants hastily.]

FIRST SERVANT
Sacred God, where are we to go to for grub and good lying to-night?
What are ill-used men to do?

SECOND SERVANT
I trudge like the rest. All the true philosophers are gone, and the middling true are going. I made up my mind like the truest that ever was as soon as I heard the general alarm beat.

THIRD SERVANT
I stay here. No Allies are going to tickle our skins. The storm which roots—Dost know what a metaphor is, comrade? I brim with them at this historic time!

SECOND SERVANT
A weapon of war used by the Cossacks?

THIRD SERVANT
Your imagination will be your ruin some day, my man! It happens to be a weapon of wisdom used by me. My metaphor is one may'st have met with on the rare times when th'hast been in good society. Here it is: The storm which roots the pine spares the p—s—b—d. Now do you see?

FIRST AND SECOND SERVANTS
Good! Your teaching, friend, is as sound as true religion! We'll not go. Hearken to what's doing outside. [Carriages are heard moving. Servants go to the window and look down.] Lord, there's the Duchess getting in. Now the Mistress of the Wardrobe; now the Ladies of the Palace; now the Prefects; now the Doctors. What a time it takes! There are near a dozen berlines, as I am a patriot! Those other carriages bear treasure. How quiet the people are! It is like a funeral procession. Not a tongue cheers her!

THIRD SERVANT
Now there will be a nice convenient time for a little good victuals and drink, and likewise pickings, before the Allies arrive, thank Mother Molly!

[From a distant part of the city bands are heard playing military marches. Guns next resound. Another servant rushes in.]

FOURTH SERVANT
Montmartre is being stormed, and bombs are falling in the Chaussee d'Antin!

[Exit fourth servant.]

THIRD SERVANT [pulling something from his hat]
Then it is time for me to gird my armour on.

SECOND SERVANT
What hast there?

[Third servant holds up a crumpled white cockade and sticks it in his hair. The firing gets louder.]

FIRST AND SECOND SERVANTS
Hast got another?

THIRD SERVANT [pulling out more]
Ay—here they are; at a price.

[The others purchase cockades of third servant. A military march is again heard. Re-enter fourth servant.]

FOURTH SERVANT
The city has capitulated! The Allied sovereigns, so it is said, will enter in grand procession to-morrow: the Prussian cavalry first, then the Austrian foot, then the Russian and Prussian foot, then the Russian horse and artillery. And to cap all, the people of Paris are glad of the change. They have put a rope round the neck of the statue of Napoleon on the column of the Grand Army, and are amusing themselves with twitching it and crying "Strangle the Tyrant!"

SECOND SERVANT
Well, well! There's rich colours in this kaleidoscopic world!

THIRD SERVANT
And there's comedy in all things—when they don't concern you.
Another glorious time among the many we've had since eighty-nine.
We have put our armour on none too soon. The Bourbons for ever!

[He leaves, followed by first and second servants.]

FOURTH SERVANT
My faith, I think I'll turn Englishman in my older years, where there's not these trying changes in the Constitution!

[Follows the others. The Allies military march waxes louder as the scene shuts.]

SCENE IV

FONTAINEBLEAU. A ROOM IN THE PALACE

[NAPOLEON is discovered walking impatiently up and down, and glancing at the clock every few minutes. Enter NEY.]

NAPOLEON [without a greeting]
Well—the result? Ah, but your looks display
A leaden dawning to the light you bring!
What—not a regency? What—not the Empress
To hold it in trusteeship for my son?

NEY

Sire, things like revolutions turn back,
But go straight on. Imperial governance
Is coffined for your family and yourself!
It is declared that military repose,
And France's well-doing, demand of you
Your abdication—unconditioned, sheer.
This verdict of the sovereigns cannot change,
And I have pushed on hot to let you know.

NAPOLEON [with repression]

I am obliged to you. You have told me promptly!—
This was to be expected. I had learnt
Of Marmont's late defection, and the Sixth's;
The consequence I easily inferred.

NEY

The Paris folk are flaked with white cockades;
Tricolors choke the kennels. Rapturously
They clamour for the Bourbons and for peace.

NAPOLEON [tartly]

I can draw inferences without assistance!

NEY [persisting]

They see the brooks of blood that have flowed forth;
They feel their own bereavements; so their mood
Asked no deep reasoning for its geniture.

NAPOLEON

I have no remarks to make on that just now.
I'll think the matter over. You shall know
By noon to-morrow my definitive.

NEY [turning to go]

I trust my saying what had to be said
Has not affronted you?

NAPOLEON [bitterly]

No; but your haste
In doing it has galled me, and has shown me
A heart that heaves no longer in my cause!
The skilled coquetting of the Government
Has nearly won you from old fellowship!...
Well; till to-morrow, marshal, then Adieu.

[Ney goes. Enter CAULAINCOURT and MACDONALD.]

Ney has got here before you; and, I deem,
Has truly told me all?

CAULAINCOURT
We thought at first
We should have had success. But fate said No;
And abdication, making no reserves,
Is, sire, we are convinced, with all respect,
The only road, if you care not to risk
The Empress; loss of every dignity,
And magnified misfortunes thrown on France.

NAPOLEON
I have heard it all; and don't agree with you.
My assets are not quite so beggarly
That I must close in such a shameful bond!
What—do you rate as naught that I am yet
Full fifty thousand strong, with Augereau,
And Soult, and Suchet true, and many more?
I still may know to play the Imperial game
As well as Alexander and his friends!
So—you will see. Where are my maps?—eh, where?
I'll trace campaigns to come! Where's my paper, ink,
To schedule all my generals and my means!

CAULAINCOURT
Sire, you have not the generals you suppose.

MACDONALD
And if you had, the mere anatomy
Of a real army, sire, that's left to you,
Must yield the war. A bad example tells.

NAPOLEON
Ah—from your manner it is worse, I see,
Than I cognize!... O Marmont, Marmont,—yours,
Yours was the bad sad lead!—I treated him
As if he were a son!—defended him,
Made him a marshal out of sheer affection,
Built, as 'twere rock, on his fidelity!
"Forsake who may," I said, "I still have him."
Child that I was, I looked for faith in friends!...

Then be it as you will. Ney's manner shows
That even he inclines to Bourbonry.—
I faint to leave France thus—curtailed, pared down
From her late spacious borders. Of the whole

This is the keenest sword that pierces me....
But all's too late: my course is closed, I see.
I'll do it—now. Call in Bertrand and Ney;
Let them be witness to my finishing!

[In much agitation he goes to the writing-table and begins drawing up a paper. BERTRAND and NEY enter; and behind them are seen through the doorway the faces of CONSTANT the valet, ROUSTAN the Mameluke, and other servants. All wait in silence till the EMPEROR has done writing. He turns in his seat without looking up.]

NAPOLEON [reading]
"It having been declared by the Allies
That the prime obstacle to Europe's peace
Is France's empery by Napoleon,
This ruler, faithful to his oath of old,
Renounces for himself and for his heirs
The throne of France and that of Italy;
Because no sacrifice, even of his life,
Is he averse to make for France's gain."
—And hereto do I sign. [He turns to the table and signs.]

[The marshals, moved, rush forward and seize his hand.]

Mark, marshals, here;
It is a conquering foe I covenant with,
And not the traitors at the Tuileries
Who call themselves the Government of France!
Caulaincourt, go to Paris as before,
Ney and Macdonald too, and hand in this
To Alexander, and to him alone.

[He gives the document, and bids them adieu almost without speech. The marshals and others go out. NAPOLEON continues sitting with his chin on his chest.

An interval of silence. There is then heard in the corridor a sound of whetting. Enter ROUSTAN the Mameluke, with a whetstone in his belt and a sword in his hand.]

ROUSTAN
After this fall, your Majesty, 'tis plain
You will not choose to live; and knowing this
I bring to you my sword.

NAPOLEON [with a nod]
I see you do, Roustan.

ROUSTAN
Will you, sire, use it on yourself,
Or shall I pass it through you?

NAPOLEON [coldly]
Neither plan
Is quite expedient for the moment, man.

ROUSTAN
Neither?

NAPOLEON
There may be, in some suited time,
Some cleaner means of carrying out such work.

ROUSTAN
Sire, you refuse? Can you support vile life
A moment on such terms? Why then, I pray,
Dispatch me with the weapon, or dismiss me.

[He holds the sword to NAPOLEON, who shakes his head.]

I live no longer under such disgrace!

[Exit ROUSTAN haughtily. NAPOLEON vents a sardonic laugh, and throws himself on a sofa, where he by and by falls asleep. The door is softly opened. ROUSTAN and CONSTANT peep in.]

CONSTANT
To-night would be as good a time to go as any. He will sleep there for hours. I have my few francs safe, and I deserve them; for I have stuck to him honourably through fourteen trying years.

ROUSTAN
How many francs have you secured?

CONSTANT
Well—more than you can count in one breath, or even two.

ROUSTAN
Where?

CONSTANT
In a hollow tree in the Forest. And as for YOUR reward, you can easily get the keys of that cabinet, where there are more than enough francs to equal mine. He will not have them, and you may as well take them as strangers.

ROUSTAN
It is not money that I want, but honour. I leave, because I can no longer stay with self-respect.

CONSTANT
And I because there is no other such valet in the temperate zone, and it is for the good of society that I should not be wasted here.

ROUSTAN
Well, as you propose going this evening I will go with you, to lend a symmetry to the drama of our departure. Would that I had served a more sensitive master! He sleeps there quite indifferent to the dishonour of remaining alive!

[NAPOLEON shows signs of waking. CONSTANT and ROUSTAN disappear. NAPOLEON slowly sits up.]

NAPOLEON
Here the scene lingers still! Here linger I!...
Things could not have gone on as they were going;
I am amazed they kept their course so long.
But long or short they have ended now—at last!
[Footsteps are heard passing through the court without.]
Hark at them leaving me! So politic rats
Desert the ship that's doomed. By morrow-dawn
I shall not have a man to shake my bed
Or say good-morning to!

SPIRIT OF THE YEARS
Herein behold
How heavily grinds the Will upon his brain,
His halting hand, and his unlighted eye.

SPIRIT IRONIC
A picture this for kings and subjects too!

SPIRIT OF THE PITIES
Yet is it but Napoleon who has failed.
The pale pathetic peoples still plod on
Through hoodwinkings to light!

NAPOLEON [rousing himself]
This now must close.
Roustan misunderstood me, though his hint
Serves as a fillip to a flaccid brain....
—How gild the sunset sky of majesty
Better than by the act esteemed of yore?
Plutarchian heroes outstayed not their fame,
And what nor Brutus nor Themistocles
Nor Cato nor Mark Antony survived,
Why, why should I? Sage Canabis, you primed me!

[He unlocks a case, takes out a little bag containing a phial, pours from it a liquid into a glass, and drinks. He then lies down and falls asleep again.

Re-enter CONSTANT softly with a bunch of keys in his hand. On his way to the cabinet he turns and looks at NAPOLEON. Seeing the glass and a strangeness in the EMPEROR, he abandons his object, rushes out, and is heard calling.

Enter MARET and BERTRAND.]

BERTRAND [shaking the Emperor]
What is the matter, sire? What's this you've done?

NAPOLEON [with difficulty]
Why did you interfere!—But it is well;
Call Caulaincourt. I'd speak with him a trice
Before I pass.

[MARET hurries out. Enter IVAN the physician, and presently

CAULAINCOURT.]
Ivan, renew this dose;
'Tis a slow workman, and requires a fellow;
Age has impaired its early promptitude.

[Ivan shakes his head and rushes away distracted. CAULAINCOURT seizes NAPOLEON'S hand.]

CAULAINCOURT
Why should you bring this cloud upon us now!

NAPOLEON
Restrain your feelings. Let me die in peace.—
My wife and son I recommend to you;
Give her this letter, and the packet there.
Defend my memory, and protect their lives.

[They shake him. He vomits.]

CAULAINCOURT
He's saved—for good or ill-as may betide!

NAPOLEON
God—here how difficult it is to die:
How easy on the passionate battle-plain!

[They open a window and carry him to it. He mends.]

Fate has resolved what man could not resolve.
I must live on, and wait what Heaven may send!

[MACDONALD and other marshals re-enter. A letter is brought from MARIE LOUISE. NAPOLEON reads it, and becomes more animated.

They are well; and they will join me in my exile.
Yes: I will live! The future who shall spell?
My wife, my son, will be enough for me.—
And I will give my hours to chronicling
In stately words that stir futurity
The might of our unmatched accomplishments;
And in the tale immortalize your names
By linking them with mine.

[He soon falls into a convalescent sleep. The marshals, etc. go out. The room is left in darkness.]

SCENE V

BAYONNE. THE BRITISH CAMP

[The foreground is an elevated stretch of land, dotted over in rows with the tents of the peninsular army. On a parade immediately beyond the tents the infantry are drawn up, awaiting something. Still farther back, behind a brook, are the French soldiery, also ranked in the same manner of reposeful expectation. In the middle-distance we see the town of Bayonne, standing within its zigzag fortifications at the junction of the river Adour with the Nive.

On the other side of the Adour rises the citadel, a fortified angular structure standing detached. A large and brilliant tricolor flag is waving indolently from a staff on the summit. The Bay of Biscay, into which the Adour flows, is seen on the left horizon as a level line.

The stillness observed by the soldiery of both armies, and by everything else in the scene except the flag, is at last broken by the firing of a signal-gun from a battery in the town-wall. The eyes of the thousands present rivet themselves on the citadel. Its waving tricolor moves down the flagstaff and disappears.]

THE REGIMENTS [unconsciously]
Ha-a-a-a!

[In a few seconds there shoots up the same staff another flag—one intended to be white; but having apparently been folded away a long time, it is mildewed and dingy.

From all the guns on the city fortifications a salute peals out. This is responded to by the English infantry and artillery with a feu-de-joie.]

THE REGIMENTS
Hurrah-h-h-h!

[The various battalions are then marched away in their respective directions and dismissed to their tents. The Bourbon standard is hoisted everywhere beside those of England, Spain, and Portugal. The scene shuts.]

SCENE VI

A HIGHWAY IN THE OUTSKIRTS OF AVIGNON

[The Rhone, the old city walls, the Rocher des Doms and its edifices, appear at the back plane of the scene under the grey light of dawn. In the foreground several postillions and ostlers with relays of horses are waiting by the roadside, gazing northward and listening for sounds. A few loungers have assembled.]

FIRST POSTILLION
He ought to be nigh by this time. I should say he'd be very glad to get this here Isle of Elba, wherever it may be, if words be true that he's treated to such ghastly compliments on's way!

SECOND POSTILLION
Blast-me-blue, I don't care what happens to him! Look at Joachim Murat, him that's made King of Naples; a man who was only in the same line of life as ourselves, born and bred in Cahors, out in Perigord, a poor little whindling place not half as good as our own. Why should he have been lifted up to king's anointment, and we not even have had a rise in wages? That's what I say.

FIRST POSTILLION
But now, I don't find fault with that dispensation in particular. It was one of our calling that the Emperor so honoured, after all, when he might have anointed a tinker, or a ragman, or a street woman's pensioner even. Who knows but that we should have been king's too, but for my crooked legs and your running pole-wound?

SECOND POSTILLION
We kings? Kings of the underground country, then, by this time, if we hadn't been too rotten-fleshed to follow the drum. However, I'll think over your defence, and I don't mind riding a stage with him, for that matter, to save him from them that mean mischief here. I've lost no sons by his battles, like some others we know.

[Enter a TRAVELLER on horseback.]

Any tidings along the road, sir of the Emperor Napoleon that was?

TRAVELLER
Tidings verily! He and his escort are threatened by the mob at every place they come to. A returning courier I have met tells me that at an inn a little way beyond here they have strung up his effigy to the sign-post, smeared it with blood, and placarded it "The Doom that awaits Thee!" He is much delayed by such humorous insults. I have hastened ahead to escape the uproar.

SECOND POSTILLION
I don't know that you have escaped it. The mob has been waiting up all night for him here.

MARKET-WOMAN [coming up]

I hope by the Virgin, as 'a called herself, that there'll be no riots here! Though I have not much pity for a man who could treat his wife as he did, and that's my real feeling. He might at least have kept them both on, for half a husband is better than none for poor women. But I'd show mercy to him, that's true, rather than have my stall upset, and messes in the streets wi' folks' brains, and stabbings, and I don't know what all!

FIRST POSTILLION
If we can do the horsing quietly out here, there will be none of that. He'll dash past the town without stopping at the inn where they expect to waylay him.—Hark, what's this coming?

[An approaching cortege is heard. Two couriers enter; then a carriage with NAPOLEON and BERTRAND; then others with the Commissioners of the Powers,—all on the way to Elba.

The carriages halt, and the change of horses is set about instantly. But before it is half completed BONAPARTE'S arrival gets known, and throngs of men and women armed with sticks and hammers rush out of Avignon and surround the carriages.]

POPULACE
Ogre of Corsica! Odious tyrant! Down with Nicholas!

BERTRAND [looking out of carriage]
Silence, and doff your hats, you ill-mannered devils!

POPULACE [scornfully]
Listen to him! Is that the Corsican? No; where is he? Give him up; give him up! We'll pitch him into the Rhone!

[Some cling to the wheels of NAPOLEON'S carriage, while others, more distant, throw stones at it. A stone breaks the carriage window.]

OLD WOMAN [shaking her fist]
Give me back my two sons, murderer! Give me back my children, whose flesh is rotting on the Russian plains!

POPULACE
Ay; give us back our kin—our fathers, our brothers, our sons—victims to your curst ambition!

[One of the mob seizes the carriage door-handle and tries to unfasten it. A valet of BONAPARTE'S seated on the box draws his sword and threatens to cut the man's arm off. The doors of the Commissioners' coaches open, and SIR NEIL CAMPBELL, GENERAL KOLLER, and COUNT SCHUVALOFF— The English, Austrian, and Russian Commissioners—jump out and come forward.]

CAMPBELL
Keep order, citizens! Do you not know
That the ex-Emperor is wayfaring
To a lone isle, in the Allies' sworn care,
Who have given a pledge to Europe for his safety?
His fangs being drawn, he is left powerless now

To do you further harm.

SCHUVALOFF
People of France
Can you insult so miserable a being?
He who gave laws to a cowed world stands now
At that world's beck, and asks its charity.
Cannot you see that merely to ignore him
Is the worst ignominy to tar him with,
By showing him he's no longer dangerous?

OLD WOMAN
How do we know the villain mayn't come back?
While there is life, my faith, there's mischief in him!

[Enter an officer with the Town-guard.]

OFFICER
Citizens, I am a zealot for the Bourbons,
As you well know. But wanton breach of faith
I will not brook. Retire!

[The soldiers drive back the mob and open a passage forward. The Commissioners re-enter their
carriages. NAPOLEON puts his head out of his window for a moment. He is haggard, shabbily dressed,
yellow-faced, and wild-eyed.]

NAPOLEON
I thank you, captain;
Also your soldiery: a thousand thanks!
[To Bertrand within] My God, these people of Avignon here
Are headstrong fools, like all the Provencal fold,
—I won't go through the town!

BERTRAND
We'll round it, sire;
And then, as soon as we get past the place,
You must disguise for the remainder miles.

NAPOLEON
I'll mount the white cockade if they invite me!
What does it matter if I do or don't?
In Europe all is past and over with me....
Yes—all is lost in Europe for me now!

BERTRAND
I fear so, sire.

NAPOLEON [after some moments]

But Asia waits a man,
And—who can tell?

OFFICER OF GUARD [to postillions]
Ahead now at full speed,
And slacken not till you have slipped the town.

[The postillions urge the horses to a gallop, and the carriages are out of sight in a few seconds. The scene shuts.]

SCENE VII

MALMAISON. THE EMPRESS JOSEPHINE'S BEDCHAMBER

[The walls are in white panels, with gilt mouldings, and the furniture is upholstered in white silk with needle-worked flowers. The long windows and the bed are similarly draped, and the toilet service is of gold. Through the panes appears a broad flat lawn adorned with vases and figures on pedestals, and entirely surrounded by trees—just now in their first fresh green under the morning rays of Whitsunday. The notes of an organ are audible from a chapel below, where the Pentecostal Mass is proceeding.

JOSEPHINE lies in the bed in an advanced stage of illness, the ABBE BERTRAND standing beside her. Two ladies-in-waiting are seated near. By the door into the ante-room, which is ajar, HOREAU the physician-in-ordinary and BOURDOIS the consulting physician are engaged in a low conversation.]

HOREAU
Lamoureux says that leeches would have saved her
Had they been used in time, before I came.
In that case, then, why did he wait for me?

BOURDOIS
Such whys are now too late! She is past all hope.
I doubt if aught had helped her. Not disease,
But heart-break and repinings are the blasts
That wither her long bloom. Soon we must tell
The Queen Hortense the worst, and the Viceroy.

HOREAU
Her death was made the easier task for grief
[As I regarded more than probable]
By her rash rising from a sore-sick bed
And donning thin and dainty May attire
To hail King Frederick-William and the Tsar
As banquet-guests, in the old regnant style.
A woman's innocent vanity!—but how dire.
She argued that amenities of State
Compelled the effort, since they had honoured her

By offering to come. I stood against it,
Pleaded and reasoned, but to no account.
Poor woman, what she did or did not do
Was of small moment to the State by then!
The Emperor Alexander has been kind
Throughout his stay in Paris. He came down
But yester-eve, of purpose to inquire.

BOURDOIS
Wellington is in Paris, too, I learn,
After his wasted battle at Toulouse.

HOREAU
Has his Peninsular army come with him?

BOURDOIS
I hear they have shipped it to America,
Where England has another war on hand.
We have armies quite sufficient here already—
Plenty of cooks for Paris broth just now!
—Come, call we Queen Hortense and Prince Eugene.

[Exeunt physicians. The ABBE BERTRAND also goes out. JOSEPHINE murmurs faintly.]

FIRST LADY [going to the bedside]
I think I heard you speak, your Majesty?

JOSEPHINE
I asked what hour it was—if dawn or eve?

FIRST LADY
Ten in the morning, Madame. You forget
You asked the same but a brief while ago.

JOSEPHINE
Did I? I thought it was so long ago!...
I wish to go to Elba with him so much,
But the Allies prevented me. And why?
I would not have disgraced him, or themselves!
I would have gone to him at Fontainebleau,
With my eight horses and my household train
In dignity, and quitted him no more....
Although I am his wife no longer now,
I think I should have gone in spite of them,
Had I not feared perversions might be sown
Between him and the woman of his choice
For whom he sacrificed me.

SECOND LADY
It is more
Than she thought fit to do, your Majesty.

JOSEPHINE
Perhaps she was influenced by her father's ire,
Or diplomatic reasons told against her.
And yet I was surprised she should allow
Aught secondary on earth to hold her from
A husband she has outwardly, at least,
Declared attachment to.

FIRST LADY
Especially,
With ever one at hand—his son and hers—
Reminding her of him.

JOSEPHINE
Yes.... Glad am I
I saw that child of theirs, though only once.
But—there was not full truth—not quite, I fear—
In what I told the Emperor that day
He led him to me at Bagatelle,
That 'twas the happiest moment of my life.
I ought not to have said it. No! Forsooth
My feeling had too, too much gall in it
To let truth shape like that!—I also said
That when my arms were round him I forgot
That I was not his mother. So spoke I,
But oh me,—I remembered it too well!—
He was a lovely child; in his fond prate
His father's voice was eloquent. One might say
I am well punished for my sins against him!

SECOND LADY
You have harmed no creature, madame; much less him!

JOSEPHINE
O but you don't quite know!... My coquetries
In our first married years nigh racked him through.
I cannot think how I could wax so wicked!...
He begged me come to him in Italy,
But I liked flirting in fair Paris best,
And would not go. The independent spouse
At that time was myself; but afterwards
I grew to be the captive, he the free.
Always 'tis so: the man wins finally!
My faults I've ransomed to the bottom sou

If ever a woman did!... I'll write to him—
I must—again, so that he understands.
Yes, I'll write now. Get me a pen and paper.

FIRST LADY [to Second Lady]
'Tis futile! She is too far gone to write;
But we must humour her.

[They fetch writing materials. On returning to the bed they find her motionless. Enter EUGENE and
QUEEN HORTENSE. Seeing the state their mother is in, they fall down on their knees by her bed.

JOSEPHINE recognizes them and smiles. Anon she is able to speak again.]

JOSEPHINE [faintly]
I am dying, dears;
And do not mind it—notwithstanding that
I feel I die regretted. You both love me!—
And as for France, I ever have desired
Her welfare, as you know—have wrought all things
A woman's scope could reach to forward it....
And to you now who watch my ebbing here,
Declare I that Napoleon's first-chose wife
Has never caused her land a needless tear.
Tell him—these things I have said—bear him my love—
Tell him—I could not write!

[An interval. She spasmodically flings her arms over her son and daughter, lets them fall, and becomes
unconscious. They fetch a looking-glass, and find that her breathing has ceased. The clock of the
Chateau strikes noon. The scene is veiled.]

SCENE VIII

LONDON. THE OPERA HOUSE

[The house is lighted up with a blaze of wax candles, and a State performance is about to begin in
honour of the Allied sovereigns now on a visit to England to celebrate the Peace. Peace-devices adorn
the theatre. A band can be heard in the street playing "The White Cockade."

An extended Royal box has been formed by removing the partitions of adjoining boxes. It is empty as
yet, but the other parts of the house are crowded to excess, and somewhat disorderly, the interior
doors having been broken down by besiegers, and many people having obtained admission without
payment. The prevalent costume of the ladies is white satin and diamonds, with a few in lilac.

The curtain rises on the first act of the opera of "Aristodemo," MADAME GRASSINI and SIGNOR
TRAMEZZINI being the leading voices. Scarcely a note of the performance can be heard amid the
exclamations of persons half suffocated by the pressure.

At the end of the first act there follows a divertissement. The curtain having fallen, a silence of expectation succeeds. It is a little past ten o'clock.

Enter the Royal box the PRINCE REGENT, accompanied by the EMPEROR OF RUSSIA, demonstrative in manner now as always, the KING OF PRUSSIA, with his mien of reserve, and many minor ROYAL PERSONAGES of Europe. There are moderate acclamations. At their back and in neighbouring boxes LORD LIVERPOOL, LORD CASTLEREAGH, officers in the suite of the sovereigns, interpreters, and others take their places.

The curtain rises again, and the performers are discovered drawn up in line on the stage. They sing "God save the King." The sovereigns stand up, bow, and resume their seats amid more applause.]

A VOICE [from the gallery]
Prinny, where's your wife? [Confusion.]

EMPEROR OF RUSSIA [to Regent]
To which of us is the inquiry addressed, Prince?

PRINCE REGENT
To you, sire, depend upon't—by way of compliment.

[The second act of the Opera proceeds.]

EMPEROR OF RUSSIA
Any later news from Elba, sir?

PRINCE REGENT
Nothing more than rumours, which, 'pon my honour, I can hardly credit. One is that Bonaparte's valet has written to say the ex-Emperor is becoming imbecile, and is an object of ridicule to the inhabitants of the island.

KING OF PRUSSIA
A blessed result, sir, if true. If he is not imbecile he is worse —planning how to involve Europe in another way. It was a short-sighted policy to offer him a home so near as to ensure its becoming a hot-bed of intrigue and conspiracy in no long time!

PRINCE REGENT
The ex-Empress, Marie-Louise, hasn't joined him after all, I learn.
Has she remained at Schonbrunn since leaving France, sires?

EMPEROR OF RUSSIA
Yes, sir; with her son. She must never go back to France. Metternich and her father will know better than let her do that. Poor young thing, I am sorry for her all the same. She would have joined Napoleon if she had been left to herself.—And I was sorry for the other wife, too. I called at Malmaison a few days before she died. A charming woman! SHE would have gone to Elba or to the devil with him. Twenty thousand people crowded down from Paris to see her lying in state last week.

PRINCE REGENT
Pity she didn't have a child by him, by God.

KING OF PRUSSIA
I don't think the other one's child is going to trouble us much.
But I wish Bonaparte himself had been sent farther away.

PRINCE REGENT
Some of our Government wanted to pack him off to St. Helena—an island somewhere in the Atlantic, or Pacific, or Great South Sea. But they were over-ruled. 'Twould have been a surer game.

EMPEROR OF RUSSIA
One hears strange stories of his saying and doings. Some of my people were telling me to-day that he says it is to Austria that he really owes his fall, and that he ought to have destroyed her when he had her in his power.

PRINCE REGENT
Dammy, sire, don't ye think he owes his fall to his ambition to humble England by rupture of the Peace of Amiens, and trying to invade us, and wasting his strength against us in the Peninsula?

EMPEROR OF RUSSIA
I incline to think, with the greatest deference, that it was Moscow that broke him.

KING OF PRUSSIA
The rejection of my conditions in the terms of peace at Prague, sires, was the turning-point towards his downfall.

[Enter a box on the opposite side of the house the PRINCESS OF WALES, attended by LADY CHARLOTTE CAMPBELL, SIR W. GELL, and others. Louder applause now rings through the theatre, drowning the sweet voice of the GRASSINI in "Aristodemo."]

LADY CHARLOTTE CAMPBELL
It is meant for your Royal Highness!

PRINCESS OF WALES
I don't think so, my dear. Punch's wife is nobody when Punch himself is present.

LADY CHARLOTTE CAMPBELL
I feel convinced that it is by their looking this way.

SIR W. GELL
Surely ma'am you will acknowledge their affection? Otherwise we may be hissed.

PRINCESS OF WALES
I know my business better than to take that morsel out of my husband's mouth. There—you see he enjoys it! I cannot assume that it is meant for me unless they call my name.

[The PRINCE REGENT rises and bows, the TSAR and the KING OF PRUSSIA doing the same.]

LADY CHARLOTTE CAMPBELL
He and the others are bowing for you, ma'am!

PRINCESS OF WALES
Mine God, then; I will bow too! [She rises and bends to them.]

PRINCE REGENT
She thinks we rose on her account.—A damn fool. [Aside.]

EMPEROR OF RUSSIA
What—didn't we? I certainly rose in homage to her.

PRINCE REGENT
No, sire. We were supposed to rise to the repeated applause of the people.

EMPEROR OF RUSSIA
H'm. Your customs sir, are a little puzzling.... [To the King of Prussia.] A fine-looking woman! I must call upon the Princess of Wales to-morrow.

KING OF PRUSSIA
I shall, at any rate, send her my respects by my chamberlain.

PRINCE REGENT [stepping back to Lord Liverpool]
By God, Liverpool, we must do something to stop 'em! They don't know what a laughing-stock they'll make of me if they go to her. Tell 'em they had better not.

LIVERPOOL
I can hardly tell them now, sir, while we are celebrating the Peace and Wellington's victories.

PRINCE REGENT
Oh, damn the peace, and damn the war, and damn Boney, and damn Wellington's victories!—the question is, how am I to get over this infernal woman!—Well, well,—I must write, or send Tyrwhitt to-morrow morning, begging them to abandon the idea of visiting her for politic reasons.

[The Opera proceeds to the end, and is followed by a hymn and chorus laudatory to peace. Next a new ballet by MONSIEUR VESTRIS, in which M. ROZIER and MADAME ANGIOLINI dance a pas-de-deux. Then the Sovereigns leave the theatre amid more applause.

The pit and gallery now call for the PRINCESS OF WALES unmistakably.

She stand up and is warmly acclaimed, returning three stately curtseys.]

A VOICE
Shall we burn down Carlton House, my dear, and him in it?

PRINCESS OF WALES
No, my good folks! Be quiet. Go home to your beds, and let me do the same.

[After some difficulty she gets out of the house. The people thin away. As the candle-snuffers extinguish the lights a shouting is heard without.]

VOICES OF CROWD
Long life to the Princess of Wales! Three cheers for a woman wronged!

[The Opera-house becomes lost in darkness.]

ACT FIFTH

SCENE I

ELBA. THE QUAY, PORTO FERRAJO

[Night descends upon a beautiful blue cove, enclosed on three sides by mountains. The port lies towards the western [right-hand] horn of the concave, behind it being the buildings of the town; their long white walls and rows of windows rise tier above tier on the steep incline at the back, and are intersected by narrow alleys and flights of steps that lead up to forts on the summit.

Upon a rock between two of these forts stands the Palace of the Mulini, NAPOLEONS'S residence in Ferrajo. Its windows command the whole town and the port.]

CHORUS OF IRONIC SPIRITS [aerial music]
The Congress of Vienna sits,
And war becomes a war of wits,
Where every Power perpends withal
Its dues as large, its friends' as small;
Till Priests of Peace prepare once more
To fight as they have fought before!

In Paris there is discontent;
Medals are wrought that represent
One now unnamed. Men whisper, "He
Who once has been, again will be!"

DUMB SHOW
Under cover of the dusk there assembles in the bay a small flotilla comprising a brig called l'Inconstant and several lesser vessels.

SPIRIT OF RUMOUR
The guardian on behalf of the Allies
Absents himself from Elba. Slow surmise
Too vague to pen, too actual to ignore,
Have strained him hour by hour, and more and more.

He takes the sea to Florence, to declare
His doubts to Austria's ministrator there.

SPIRIT IRONIC
When he returns, Napoleon will be—where?

Boats put off from these ships to the quay, where are now discovered to have silently gathered a body of grenadiers of the Old Guard. The faces of DROUOT and CAMBRONNE are revealed by the occasional fleck of a lantern to be in command of them. They are quietly taken aboard the brig, and a number of men of different arms to the other vessels.

CHORUS OF RUMOURS [aerial music]
Napoleon is going,
And nought will prevent him;
He snatches the moment
Occasion has lent him!

And what is he going for,
Worn with war's labours?
—To reconquer Europe
With seven hundred sabres.

About eight o'clock we observe that the windows of the Palace of the Mulini are lighted and open, and that two women sit at them: the EMPEROR'S mother and the PRINCESS PAULINE. They wave adieux to some one below, and in a short time a little open low-wheeled carriage, drawn by the PRINCESS PAULINE'S two ponies, descends from the house to the port. The crowd exclaims "The Emperor!" NAPOLEON appears in his grey great-coat, and is much fatter than when he left France. BERTRAND sits beside him.

He quickly alights and enters the waiting boat. It is a tense moment. As the boat rows off the sailors sing the Marseillaise, and the gathered inhabitants join in. When the boat reaches the brig its sailors join in also, and shout "Paris or death!" Yet the singing has a melancholy cadence. A gun fires as a signal of departure. The night is warm and balmy for the season. Not a breeze is there to stir a sail, and the ships are motionless.

CHORUS OF RUMOURS
Haste is salvation;
And still he stays waiting:
The calm plays the tyrant,
His venture belating!

Should the corvette return
With the anxious Scotch colonel,
Escape would be frustrate,
Retention eternal.

Four aching hours are spent thus. NAPOLEON remains silent on the deck, looking at the town lights, whose reflections bore like augers into the water of the bay. The sails hang flaccidly. Then a feeble breeze, then a strong south wind, begins to belly the sails; and the vessels move.

CHORUS OF RUMOURS
The south wind, the south wind,
The south wind will save him,
Embaying the frigate
Whose speed would enslave him;
Restoring the Empire
That fortune once gave him!
The moon rises and the ships silently disappear over the horizon
as it mounts higher into the sky.

SCENE II

VIENNA. THE IMPERIAL PALACE

[The fore-part of the scene is the interior of a dimly lit gallery with an openwork screen or grille on one side of it that commands a bird's-eye view of the grand saloon below. At present the screen is curtained. Sounds of music and applause in the saloon ascend into the gallery, and an irradiation from the same quarter shines up through chinks in the curtains of the grille.

Enter the gallery MARIE LOUISE and the COUNTESS OF BRIGNOLE, followed by the COUNT NEIPPERG, a handsome man of forty two with a bandage over one eye.]

COUNTESS OF BRIGNOLE
Listen, your Majesty. You gather all
As well as if you moved amid them there,
And are advantaged with free scope to flit
The moment the scene palls.

MARIE LOUISE
Ah, my dear friend,
To put it so is flower-sweet of you;
But a fallen Empress, doomed to furtive peeps
At scenes her open presence would unhinge,
Reads not much interest in them! Yet, in truth,
'Twas gracious of my father to arrange
This glimpse-hole for my curiosity.
—But I must write a letter ere I look;
You can amuse yourself with watching them.—
Count, bring me pen and paper. I am told
Madame de Montesquiou has been distressed
By some alarm; I write to ask its shape.

[NEIPPERG spreads writing materials on a table, and MARIE LOUISE sits. While she writes he stays near her. MADAME DE BRIGNOLE goes to the screen and parts the curtains.

The light of a thousand candles blazes up into her eyes from below. The great hall is decorated in white and silver, enriched by evergreens and flowers. At the end a stage is arranged, and Tableaux Vivants are in progress thereon, representing the history of the House of Austria, in which figure the most charming women of the Court.

There are present as spectators nearly all the notables who have assembled for the Congress, including the EMPEROR OF AUSTRIA himself, has gay wife, who quite eclipses him, the EMPEROR ALEXANDER, the KING OF PRUSSIA—still in the mourning he has never abandoned since the death of QUEEN LUISA,—the KING OF BAVARIA and his son, METTERNICH, TALLEYRAND, WELLINGTON, NESSELRODE, HARDENBERG; and minor princes, ministers, and officials of all nations.]

COUNTESS OF BRIGNOLE [suddenly from he grille]
Something has happened—so it seems, madame!
The Tableau gains no heed from them, and all
Turn murmuring together.

MARIE LOUISE
What may be?

[She rises with languid curiosity, and COUNT NEIPPERG adroitly takes her hand and leads her forward. All three look down through the grille.]

NEIPPERG
some strange news, certainly, your Majesty,
Is being discussed.—I'll run down and inquire.

MARIE LOUISE [playfully]
Nay—stay here. We shall learn soon enough.

NEIPPERG
Look at their faces now. Count Metternich
Stares at Prince Talleyrand—no muscle moving.
The King of Prussia blinks bewilderedly
Upon Lord Wellington.

MARIE LOUISE [concerned]
Yes; so it seems....
They are thunderstruck. See, though the music beats,
The ladies of the Tableau leave their place,
And mingle with the rest, and quite forget
That they are in masquerade. The sovereigns show
By far the gravest mien.... I wonder, now,
If it has aught to do with me or mine?
Disasters mostly have to do with me!

COUNTESS OF BRIGNOLE
Those rude diplomists from England there,
At your Imperial father's consternation,
And Russia's, and the King of Prussia's gloom,
Shake shoulders with hid laughter! That they call
The English sense of humour, I infer,—
To see a jest in other people's troubles!

MARIE LOUISE [hiding her presages]
They ever take things thus phlegmatically:
The safe sea minimizes Continental scare
In their regard. I wish it did in mine!
But Wellington laughs not, as I discern.

NEIPPERG
Perhaps, though fun for the other English here,
It means new work for him. Ah—notice now
The music makes no more pretence to play!
Sovereigns and ministers have moved apart,
And talk, and leave the ladies quite aloof—
Even the Grand Duchesses and Empress, all—
Such mighty cogitations trance their minds!

MARIE LOUISE [with more anxiety]
Poor ladies; yea, they draw into the rear,
And whisper ominous words among themselves!
Count Neipperg—I must ask you now—go glean
What evil lowers. I am riddled through
With strange surmises and more strange alarms!

[The COUNTESS OF MONTESQUIOU enters.]

Ah—we shall learn it now. Well—what, madame?

COUNTESS OF MONTESQUIOU [breathlessly]
Your Majesty, the Emperor Napoleon
Has vanished from Elba! Wither flown,
And how, and why, nobody says or knows.

MARIE LOUISE [sinking into a chair]
My divination pencilled on my brain
Something not unlike that! The rigid mien
That mastered Wellington suggested it....
Complicity will be ascribed to me,
Unwitting though I stand!... [A pause.]
He'll not succeed!
And my fair plans for Parma will be marred,
And my son's future fouled!—I must go hence,

And instantly declare to Metternich
That I know nought of this; and in his hands
Place me unquestioningly, with dumb assent
To serve the Allies.... Methinks that I was born
Under an evil-coloured star, whose ray
Darts death at joys!—Take me away, Count.—You [to the ladies]
Can stay and see the end.

[Exeunt MARIE LOUISE and NEIPPERG. MESDAMES DE MONTESQUIOU and DE BRIGNOLE go to the grille and watch and listen.]

VOICE OF ALEXANDER [below]
I told you, Prince, that it would never last!

VOICE OF TALLEYRAND
Well, sire, you should have sent him to the Azores,
Or the Antilles, or best, Saint-Helena.

VOICE OF THE KING OF PRUSSIA
Instead, we send him but two days from France,
Give him an island as his own domain,
A military guard of large resource,
And millions for his purse!

ANOTHER VOICE
The immediate cause
Must be a negligence in watching him.
The British Colonel Campbell should have seen
That apertures for flight were wired and barred
To such a cunning bird!

ANOTHER VOICE
By all report
He took the course direct to Naples Bay.

VOICES [of new arrivals]
He has made his way to France—so all tongues tell—
And landed there, at Cannes! [Excitement.]

COUNTESS OF BRIGNOLE
Do now but note
How cordial intercourse resolves itself
To sparks of sharp debate! The lesser guests
Are fain to steal unnoticed from a scene
Wherein they feel themselves as surplusage
Beside the official minds.—I catch a sign
The King of Prussia makes the English Duke;
They leave the room together.

COUNTESS OF MONTESQUIOU
Yes; wit wanes,
And all are going—Prince Talleyrand,
The Emperor Alexander, Metternich,
The Emperor Francis.... So much for the Congress!
Only a few blank nobodies remain,
And they seem terror-stricken.... Blackly ends
Such fair festivities. The red god War
Stalks Europe's plains anew!

[The curtain of the grille is dropped. MESDAMES DE MONTESQUIOU and DE BRIGNOLE leave the gallery.
The light is extinguished there and the scene disappears.]

SCENE III

LA MURE, NEAR GRENOBLE

[A lonely road between a lake and some hills, two or three miles outside the village of la Mure, is
discovered. A battalion of the Fifth French royalist regiment of the line under COMMANDANT LESSARD,
is drawn up in the middle of the road with a company of sappers and miners, comprising altogether
about eight hundred men.

Enter to them from the south a small detachment of lancers with an aide-de-camp at their head. They
ride up to within speaking distance.]

LESSARD
They are from Bonaparte. Present your arms!

AIDE [calling]
We'd parley on Napoleon's behalf,
And fain would ask you join him.

LESSARD
Al parole
With rebel bands the Government forbids.
Come five steps further and we fire!

AIDE
To France,
And to posterity through fineless time,
Must you then answer for so foul a blow
Against the common weal!

[NAPOLEON'S aide-de-camp and the lancers turn about and ride back out of sight. The royalist troops
wait. Presently there reappears from the same direction a small column of soldiery, representing the

whole of NAPOLEON'S little army shipped from Elba. It is divided into an advance-guard under COLONEL MALLET, and two bodies behind, a troop of Polish lancers under COLONEL JERMANWSKI on the right side of the road, and some officers without troops on the left, under MAJOR PACCONI.

NAPOLEON rides in the midst of the advance-guard, in the old familiar "redingote grise," cocked hat, and tricolor cockade, his well-known profile keen against the hills. He is attended by GENERALS BERTRAND, DROUOT, and CAMBRONNE. When they get within gun-shot of the royalists the men are halted. NAPOLEON dismounts and steps forward.]

NAPOLEON
Direct the men
To lodge their weapons underneath the arm,
Points downward. I shall not require them here.

COLONEL MALLET
Sire, is it not a needless jeopardy
To meet them thus? The sentiments of these
We do not know, and the first trigger pressed
May end you.

NAPOLEON
I have thought it out, my friend,
And value not my life as in itself,
But as to France, severed from whose embrace]
I am dead already.

[He repeats the order, which is carried out. There is a breathless silence, and people from the village gather round with tragic expectations. NAPOLEON walks on alone towards the Fifth battalion, Throwing open his great-coat and revealing his uniform and the ribbon of the Legion of Honour. Raising his hand to his hat he salutes.]

LESSARD
Present arms!

[The firelocks of the royalist battalion are levelled at NAPOLEON.]

NAPOLEON [still advancing]
Men of the Fifth,
See—here I am!... Old friends, do you not know me?
If there be one among you who would slay
His Chief of proud past years, let him come on
And do it now!

[A pause.]

LESSARD [to his next officer]
They are death-white at his words!
They'll fire not on this man. And I am helpless.

SOLDIERS [suddenly]
Why yes! We know you, father. Glad to see ye!
The Emperor for ever! Ha! Huzza!

[They throw their arms upon the ground, and, rushing forward, sink down and seize NAPOLEON'S knees and kiss his hands. Those who cannot get near him wave their shakos and acclaim him passionately. BERTRAND, DROUOT, and CAMBRONNE come up.]

NAPOLEON [privately]
All is accomplished, Bertrand! Ten days more,
And we are snug within the Tuileries.

[The soldiers tear out their white cockades and trample on them, and disinter from the bottom of their knapsacks tricolors, which they set up.

NAPOLEON'S own men now arrive, and fraternize with and embrace the soldiers of the Fifth. When the emotion has subsided, NAPOLEON forms the whole body into a square and addresses them.]

Soldiers, I came with these few faithful ones
To save you from the Bourbons,—treasons, tricks,
Ancient abuses, feudal tyranny—
From which I once of old delivered you.
The Bourbon throne is illegitimate
Because not founded on the nation's will,
But propped up for the profit of a few.
Comrades, is this not so?

A GRENADIER
Yes, verily, sire.
You are the Angel of the Lord to us;
We'll march with you to death or victory! [Shouts.]

[At this moment a howling dog crosses in front of them with a cockade tied to its tail. The soldiery of both sides laugh loudly.

NAPOLEON forms both bodies of troops into one column. Peasantry run up with buckets of sour wine and a single glass; NAPOLEON takes his turn with the rank and file in drinking from it. He bids the whole column follow him to Grenoble and Paris.

Exeunt soldiers headed by NAPOLEON. The scene shuts.]

SCENE IV

SCHONBRUNN

[The gardens of the Palace. Fountains and statuary are seen around, and the Gloriette colonnade rising against the sky on a hill behind.

The ex-EMPRESS MARIE LOUISE is discovered walking up and down. Accompanying her is the KING OF ROME—now a blue-eye, fair-haired child—in the charge of the COUNTESS OF MONTESQUIOU. Close by is COUNT NEIPPERG, and at a little distance MENEVAL, her attendant and Napoleon's adherent.

The EMPEROR FRANCIS and METTERNICH enter at the other end of the parterre.]

MARIE LOUISE [with a start]
Here are the Emperor and Prince Metternich.
Wrote you as I directed?

NEIPPERG
Promptly so.
I said your Majesty had not part
In this mad move of your Imperial spouse,
And made yourself a ward of the Allies;
Adding, that you had vowed irrevocably
To enter France no more.

MARIE LOUISE
Your worthy zeal
Has been a trifle swift. My meaning stretched
Not quite so far as that.... And yet—and yet
It matters little. Nothing matters much!

[The EMPEROR and METTERNICH come forward. NEIPPERG retires.]

FRANCIS
My daughter, you did not a whit too soon
Voice your repudiation. Have you seen
What the allies have papered Europe with?

MARIE LOUISE
I have seen nothing.

FRANCIS
Please you read it, Prince.

METTERNICH [taking out a paper]
"The Powers assembled at the Congress here
Owe it to their own troths and dignities,
And to the furtherance of social order,
To make a solemn Declaration, thus:
By breaking the convention as to Elba,
Napoleon Bonaparte forthwith destroys
His only legal title to exist,

And as a consequence has hurled himself
Beyond the pale of civil intercourse.
Disturber of the tranquillity of the world,
There can be neither peace nor truce with him,
And public vengeance is his self-sought doom.—
Signed by the Plenipotentiaries."

MARIE LOUISE [pale]
O God,
How terrible!... What shall—[she begins weeping.]

KING OF ROME
Is it papa
They want to hurt like that, dear Mamma 'Quiou?
Then 'twas no good my praying for him so;
And I can see that I am not going to be
A King much longer!

COUNTESS OF MONTESQUIOU   [retiring with the child]
Pray for him, Monseigneur,
Morning and evening just the same! They plan
To take you off from me. But don't forget—
Do as I say!

KING OF ROME
Yes, Mamma 'Quiou, I will!—
But why have I no pages now? And why
Does my mamma the Empress weep so much?

COUNTESS OF MONTESQUIOU
We'll talk elsewhere.

[MONTESQUIOU and the KING OF ROME withdraw to back.]

FRANCIS
At least, then, you agree
Not to attempt to follow Paris-ward
Your conscience-lacking husband, and create
More troubles in the State?—Remember this,
I sacrifice my every man and horse
Ere he Rule France again.

MARIE LOUISE
I am pledged already
To hold by the Allies; let that suffice!

METTERNICH
For the clear good of all, your Majesty,

And for your safety and the King of Rome's,
It most befits that your Imperial father
Should have sole charge of the young king henceforth,
While these convulsions rage. That this is so
You will see, I think, in view of being installed
As Parma's Duchess, and take steps therefor.

MARIE LOUISE [coldly]
I understand the terms to be as follows:
Parma is mine—my very own possession,—
And as a counterquit, the guardianship
Is ceded to my father of my son,
And I keep out of France.

METTERNICH
And likewise this:
All missives that your Majesty receives
Under Napoleon's hand, you tender straight
The Austrian Cabinet, the seals unbroke;
With those received already.

FRANCIS
You discern
How vastly to the welfare of your son
This course must tend? Duchess of Parma throned
You shine a wealthy woman, to endow
Your son with fortune and large landed fee.

MARIE LOUISE [bitterly]
I must have Parma: and those being the terms
Perforce accept! I weary of the strain
Of statecraft and political embroil:
I long for private quiet!... And now wish
To say no more at all.

[MENEVAL, who has heard her latter remarks, turns sadly away.]

FRANCIS
There's nought to say;
All is in train to work straightforwardly.

[FRANCIS and METTERNICH depart. MARIE LOUISE retires towards the child and the COUNTESS OF
MONTESQUIOU at the back of the parterre, where they are joined by NEIPPERG.

Enter in front DE MONTROND, a secret emissary of NAPOLEON, disguised as a florist examining the
gardens. MENEVAL recognizes him and comes forward.]

MENEVAL

Why are you here, de Montrond? All is hopeless!

DE MONTROND
Wherefore? The offer of the Regency
I come empowered to make, and will conduct her
Safely to Strassburg with her little son,
If she shrink not to breech her as a man,
And tiptoe from a postern unperceived?

MENEVAL
Though such quaint gear would mould her to a youth
Fair as Adonis on a hunting morn,
Yet she'll refuse! A German prudery
Sits on her still; more, kneaded by her arts
There's no will left to her. I conjured her
To hold aloof, sign nothing. But in vain.

DE MONTROND [looking towards Marie Louise]
I fain would put it to her privately!

MENEVAL
A thing impossible. No word to her
Without a word to him you see with her,
Neipperg to wit. She grows indifferent
To dreams as Regent; visioning a future
Wherein her son and self are two of three
But where the third is not Napoleon.

DE MONTROND [In sad surprise]
I may as well go hence then as I came,
And kneel to Heaven for one thing—that success
Attend Napoleon in the coming throes!

MENEVAL
I'll walk with you for safety to the gate,
Though I am as the Emperor's man suspect,
And any day may be dismissed. If so
I go to Paris.

[Exeunt MENEVAL and DE MONTROND.]

SPIRIT IRONIC
Had he but persevered, and biassed her
To slip the breeches on, and hie away,
Who knows but that the map of France had shaped
And it will never now!

[There enters from the other side of the gardens MARIA CAROLINA, ex-Queen of Naples, and grandmother of Marie Louise. The latter, dismissing MONTESQUIOU and the child, comes forward.]

MARIA CAROLINA
I have crossed from Hetzendorf to kill an hour;
Why art so pensive, dear?

MARIE LOUISE
Ah, why! My lines
Rule ruggedly. You doubtless have perused
This vicious cry against the Emperor?
He's outlawed—to be caught alive or dead,
Like any noisome beast!

MARIA CAROLINA
Nought have I heard,
My child. But these vile tricks, to pluck you from
Your nuptial plightage and your rightful glory
Make me belch oaths!—You shall not join your husband
Do they assert? My God, I know one thing,
Outlawed or no, I'd knot my sheets forthwith,
Were I but you, and steal to him in disguise,
Let come what would come! Marriage is for life.

MARIE LOUISE
Mostly; not always: not with Josephine;
And, maybe, not with me. But, that apart,
I could do nothing so outrageous.
Too many things, dear grand-dame, you forget.
A puppet I, by force inflexible,
Was bid to wed Napoleon at a nod,—
The man acclaimed to me from cradle-days
As the incarnate of all evil things,
The Antichrist himself.—I kissed the cup,
Gulped down the inevitable, and married him;
But none the less I saw myself therein
The lamb whose innocent flesh was dressed to grace
The altar of dynastic ritual!—
Hence Elba flung no duty-call to me,
Neither does Paris now.

MARIA CAROLINA
I do perceive
They have worked on you to much effect already!
Go, join your Count; he waits you, dear.—Well, well;
The way the wind blows needs no cock to tell!

[Exeunt severally QUEEN MARIA CAROLINA and MARIE LOUISE with NEIPPERG. The sun sets over the gardens and the scene fades.]

SCENE V

LONDON. THE OLD HOUSE OF COMMONS

[The interior of the Chamber appears as in Scene III., Act I., Part I., except that the windows are not open and the trees without are not yet green.

Among the Members discovered in their places are, of ministers and their supporters, LORD CASTLEREAGH the Foreign Secretary, VANSITTART Chancellor of the Exchequer, BATHURST, PALMERSTON the War Secretary, ROSE, PONSONBY, ARBUTHNOT, LUSHINGTON, GARROW the Attorney General, SHEPHERD, LONG, PLUNKETT, BANKES; and among those of the Opposition SIR FRANCIS BURDETT, WHITBREAD, TIERNEY, ABERCROMBY, DUNDAS, BRAND, DUNCANNON, LAMBTON, HEATHCOTE, SIR SAMUEL ROMILLY, G. WALPOLE, RIDLEY, OSBORNE, and HORNER.

Much interest in the debate is apparent, and the galleries are full. LORD CASTLEREAGH rises.]

CASTLEREAGH
At never a moment in my stressed career,
Amid no memory-moving urgencies,
Have I, sir, felt so gravely set on me
The sudden, vast responsibility
That I feel now. Few things conceivable
Could more momentous to the future be
Than what may spring from counsel here to-night
On means to meet the plot unparalleled
In full fierce play elsewhere. Sir, this being so,
And seeing how the events of these last days
Menace the toil of twenty anxious years,
And peril all that period's patient aim,
No auguring mind can doubt that deeds which root
In steadiest purpose only, will effect
Deliverance from a world-calamity
As dark as any in the vaults of Time.

Now, what we notice front and foremost is
That this convulsion speaks not, pictures not
The heart of France. It comes of artifice—
From the unique and sinister influence
Of a smart army-gamester—upon men
Who have shared his own excitements, spoils, and crimes.—
This man, who calls himself most impiously
The Emperor of France by Grace of God,
Has, in the scale of human character,

Dropt down so low, that he has set at nought
All pledges, stipulations, guarantees,
And stepped upon the only pedestal
On which he cares to stand—his lawless will.
Indeed, it is a fact scarce credible
That so mysteriously in his own breast
Did this adventurer lock the scheme he planned,
That his companion Bertrand, chief in trust,
Was unapprised thereof until the hour
In which the order to embark was given!

I think the House will readily discern
That the wise, wary trackway to be trod
By our own country in the crisis reached,
Must lie 'twixt two alternatives,—of war
In concert with the Continental Powers,
Or of an armed and cautionary course
Sufficing for the present phase of things.

Whatever differences of view prevail
On the so serious and impending question—
Whether in point of prudent reckoning
'Twere better let the power set up exist,
Or promptly at the outset deal with it—
Still, to all eyes it is imperative
That some mode of safeguardance be devised;
And if I cannot range before the House,
At this stage, all the reachings of the case,
I will, if needful, on some future day
Poise these nice matters on their merits here.

Meanwhile I have to move:
That an address unto His Royal Highness
Be humbly offered for his gracious message,
And to assure him that his faithful Commons
Are fully roused to the dark hazardries
To which the life and equanimity
Of Europe are exposed by deeds in France,
In contravention of the plighted pacts
At Paris in the course of yester-year.

That, in a cause of such wide-waked concern,
It doth afford us real relief to know
That concert with His Majesty's Allies
Is being effected with no loss of time—
Such concert as will thoroughly provide
For Europe's full and long security.

[Cheers.]

That we, with zeal, will speed such help to him
So to augment his force by sea and land
As shall empower him to set afoot
Swift measures meet for its accomplishing.

[Cheers.]

BURDETT
It seems to me almost impossible,
Weighing the language of the noble lord,
To catch its counsel,—whether peace of war. [Hear, hear.]
If I translate his words to signify
The high expediency of watch and ward,
That we may not be taken unawares,
I own concurrence; but if he propose
Too plunge this realm into a sea of blood
To reinstate the Bourbon line in France,
I should but poorly do my duty here
Did I not lift my voice protestingly
Against so ruinous an enterprise!

Sir, I am old enough to call to mind
The first fierce frenzies for the selfsame end,
The fruit of which was to endow this man,
The object of your apprehension now,
With such a might as could not be withstood
By all of banded Europe, till he roamed
And wrecked it wantonly on Russian plains.
Shall, then, another score of scourging years
Distract this land to make a Bourbon king?
Wrongly has Bonaparte's late course been called
A rude incursion on the soil of France.—
Who ever knew a sole and single man
Invade a nation thirty million strong,
And gain in some few days full sovereignty
Against the nation's will!—The truth is this:
The nation longed for him, and has obtained him....

I have beheld the agonies of war
Through many a weary season; seen enough
To make me hold that scarcely any goal
Is worth the reaching by so red a road.
No man can doubt that this Napoleon stands
As Emperor of France by Frenchmen's wills.
Let the French settle, then, their own affairs;
I say we shall have nought to apprehend!—

Much as I might advance in proof of this,
I'll dwell not thereon now. I am satisfied
To give the general reasons which, in brief,
Balk my concurrence in the Address proposed.

[Cheers.]

PONSONBY
My words will be but few, for the Address
Constrains me to support it as it stands.
So far from being the primary step to war,
Its sense and substance is, in my regard,
To leave the House to guidance by events
On the grave question of hostilities.

The statements of the noble lord, I hold,
Have not been candidly interpreted
By grafting on to them a headstrong will,
As does the honourable baronet,
To rob the French of Buonaparte's rule,
And force them back to Bourbon monarchism.
That our free land, at this abnormal time,
Should put her in a pose of wariness,
No unwarped mind can doubt. Must war revive,
Let it be quickly waged; and quickly, too,
Reach its effective end: though 'tis my hope,
My ardent hope, that peace may be preserved.

WHITBREAD
Were it that I could think, as does my friend,
That ambiguity of sentiment
Informed the utterance of the noble lord
[As oft does ambiguity of word],
I might with satisfied and sure resolve
Vote straight for the Address. But eyeing well
The flimsy web there woven to entrap
The credence of my honourable friends,
I must with all my energy contest
The wisdom of a new and hot crusade
For fixing who shall fill the throne of France.

Already are the seeds of mischief sown:
The Declaration at Vienna, signed
Against Napoleon, is, in my regard,
Abhorrent, and our country's character
Defaced by our subscription to its terms!
If words have any meaning it incites

To sheer assassination; it proclaims
That any meeting Bonaparte may slay him;
And, whatso language the Allies now hold,
In that outburst, at least, was war declared.
The noble lord to-night would second it,
Would seem to urge that we full arm, then wait
For just as long, no longer, than would serve
The preparations of the other Powers,
And then—pounce down on France!

CASTLEREAGH
No, no! Not so.

WHITBREAD
Good God, then, what are we to understand?—
However, this denial is a gain,
And my misapprehension owes its birth
Entirely to that mystery of phrase
Which taints all rhetoric of the noble lord,

Well, what is urged for new aggression now,
To vamp up and replace the Bourbon line?
The wittiest man who ever sat here (2) said
That half our nation's debt had been incurred
In efforts to suppress the Bourbon power,
The other half in efforts to restore it, [laughter]
And I must deprecate a further plunge
For ends so futile! Why, since Ministers
Craved peace with Bonaparte at Chatillon,
Should they refuse him peace and quiet now?

This brief amendment therefore I submit
To limit Ministers' aggressiveness
And make self-safety all their chartering:
"We at the same time earnestly implore
That the Prince Regent graciously induce
Strenuous endeavours in the cause of peace,
So long as it be done consistently
With the due honour of the English crown."

[Cheers.]

CASTLEREAGH
The arguments of Members opposite
Posit conditions which experience proves
But figments of a dream;—that honesty,
Truth, and good faith in this same Bonaparte
May be assumed and can be acted on:

This of one who is loud to violate
Bonds the most sacred, treaties the most grave!...

It follows not that since this realm was won
To treat with Bonaparte at Chatillon,
It can treat now. And as for assassination,
The sentiments outspoken here to-night
Are much more like to urge to desperate deeds
Against the persons of our good Allies,
Than are, against Napoleon, statements signed
By the Vienna plenipotentiaries!

We are, in fine, too fully warranted
On moral grounds to strike at Bonaparte,
If we at any crisis reckon it
Expedient so to do. The Government
Will act throughout in concert with the Allies,
And Ministers are well within their rights
To claim that their responsibility
Be not disturbed by hackneyed forms of speech ["Oh, oh"]
Upon war's horrors, and the bliss of peace,—
Which none denies! [Cheers.]

PONSONBY
I ask the noble lord,
If that his meaning and pronouncement be
Immediate war?

CASTLEREAGH
I have not phrased it so.

OPPOSITION CRIES
The question is unanswered!

[There are excited calls, and the House divides. The result is announced as thirty-seven for
WHITBREAD'S amendment, and against it two hundred and twenty. The clock strikes twelve as the
House adjourns.]

SCENE VI

WESSEX. DURNOVER GREEN, CASTERBRIDGE

[On a patch of green grass on Durnover Hill, in the purlieus of Casterbridge, a rough gallows has been
erected, and an effigy of Napoleon hung upon it. Under the effigy are faggots of brushwood.

It is the dusk of a spring evening, and a great crowd has gathered, comprising male and female inhabitants of the Durnover suburb and villagers from distances of many miles. Also are present some of the county yeomanry in white leather breeches and scarlet, volunteers in scarlet with green facings, and the REVEREND MR. PALMER, vicar of the parish, leaning against the post of his garden door, and smoking a clay pipe of preternatural length. Also PRIVATE CANTLE from Egdon Heath, and SOLOMON LONGWAYS of Casterbridge. The Durnover band, which includes a clarionet, {serpent,} oboe, tambourine, cymbals, and drum, is playing "Lord Wellington's Hornpipe."]

RUSTIC [wiping his face]
Says I, please God I'll lose a quarter to zee he burned! And I left Stourcastle at dree o'clock to a minute. And if I'd known that I should be too late to zee the beginning on't, I'd have lost a half to be a bit sooner.

YEOMAN
Oh, you be soon enough good-now. He's just going to be lighted.

RUSTIC
But shall I zee en die? I wanted to zee if he'd die hard,

YEOMAN
Why, you don't suppose that Boney himself is to be burned here?

RUSTIC
What—not Boney that's to be burned?

A WOMAN
Why, bless the poor man, no! This is only a mommet they've made of him, that's got neither chine nor chitlings. His innerds be only a lock of straw from Bridle's barton.

LONGWAYS
He's made, neighbour, of a' old cast jacket and breeches from our barracks here. Likeways Grammer Pawle gave us Cap'n Meggs's old Zunday shirt that she'd saved for tinder-box linnit; and Keeper Tricksey of Mellstock emptied his powder-horn into a barm-bladder, to make his heart wi'.

RUSTIC [vehemently]
Then there's no honesty left in Wessex folk nowadays at all! "Boney's going to be burned on Durnover Green to-night,"— that was what I thought, to be sure I did, that he'd been catched sailing from his islant and landed at Budmouth and brought to Casterbridge Jail, the natural retreat of malefactors!— False deceivers—making me lose a quarter who can ill afford it; and all for nothing!

LONGWAYS
'Tisn't a mo'sel o' good for thee to cry out against Wessex folk, when 'twas all thy own stunpoll ignorance.

[The VICAR OF DURNOVER removes his pipe and spits perpendicularly.]

VICAR
My dear misguided man, you don't imagine that we should be so inhuman in this Christian country as to burn a fellow creature alive?

RUSTIC
Faith, I won't say I didn't! Durnover folk have never had the highest of Christian character, come to that. And I didn't know but that even a pa'son might backslide to such things in these gory times—I won't say on a Zunday, but on a week-night like this—when we think what a blasphemious rascal he is, and that there's not a more charnel-minded villain towards womenfolk in the whole world.

[The effigy has by this time been kindled, and they watch it burn, the flames making the faces of the crowd brass-bright, and lighting the grey tower of Durnover Church hard by.]

WOMAN [singing]
Bayonets and firelocks!
I wouldn't my mammy should know't
But I've been kissed in a sentry-box,
Wrapped up in a soldier's coat!

PRIVATE CANTLE
Talk of backsliding to burn Boney, I can backslide to anything when my blood is up, or rise to anything, thank God for't! Why, I shouldn't mind fighting Boney single-handed, if so be I had the choice o' weapons, and fresh Rainbarrow flints in my flint-box, and could get at him downhill. Yes, I'm a dangerous hand with a pistol now and then!... Hark, what's that? [A horn is heard eastward on the London Road.] Ah, here comes the mail. Now we may learn something. Nothing boldens my nerves like news of slaughter!

[Enter mail-coach and steaming horses. It halts for a minute while the wheel is skidded and the horses stale.]

SEVERAL
What was the latest news from abroad, guard, when you left
Piccadilly White-Horse-Cellar!

GUARD
You have heard, I suppose, that he's given up to public vengeance, by Gover'ment orders? Anybody may take his life in any way, fair or foul, and no questions asked. But Marshal Ney, who was sent to fight him, flung his arms round his neck and joined him with all his men. Next, the telegraph from Plymouth sends news landed there by The Sparrow, that he has reached Paris, and King Louis has fled. But the air got hazy before the telegraph had finished, and the name of the place he had fled to couldn't be made out.

[The VICAR OF DURNOVER blows a cloud of smoke, and again spits perpendicularly.]

VICAR
Well, I'm d— Dear me—dear me! The Lord's will be done.

GUARD
And there are to be four armies sent against him—English, Proosian, Austrian, and Roosian: the first two under Wellington and Blucher. And just as we left London a show was opened of Boney on horseback as

large as life, hung up with his head downwards. Admission one shilling; children half-price. A truly patriot spectacle!—Not that yours here is bad for a simple country-place.

[The coach drives on down the hill, and the crowd reflectively watches the burning.]

WOMAN [singing]
I
My Love's gone a-fighting
Where war-trumpets call,
The wrongs o' men righting
Wi' carbine and ball,
And sabre for smiting,
And charger, and all

II
Of whom does he think there
Where war-trumpets call?
To whom does he drink there,
Wi' carbine and ball
On battle's red brink there,
And charger, and all?

III
Her, whose voice he hears humming
Where war-trumpets call,
"I wait, Love, thy coming
Wi' carbine and ball,
And bandsmen a-drumming
Thee, charger and all!"

[The flames reach the powder in the effigy, which is blown to rags. The band marches off playing "When War's Alarms," the crowd disperses, the vicar stands musing and smoking at his garden door till the fire goes out and darkness curtains the scene.]

ACT SIXTH

SCENE I

THE BELGIAN FRONTIER

[The village of Beaumont stands in the centre foreground of a birds'-eye prospect across the Belgian frontier from the French side, being close to the Sambre further back in the scene, which pursues a crinkled course between high banks from Maubeuge on the left to Charleroi on the right.

In the shadows that muffle all objects, innumerable bodies of infantry and cavalry are discerned bivouacking in and around the village. This mass of men forms the central column of NAPOLEONS'S army.

The right column is seen at a distance on that hand, also near the frontier, on the road leading towards Charleroi; and the left column by Solre-sur-Sambre, where the frontier and the river nearly coincide

The obscurity thins and the June dawn appears.]

DUMB SHOW
The bivouacs of the central column become broken up, and a movement ensues rightwards on Charleroi. The twelve regiments of cavalry which are in advance move off first; in half an hour more bodies move, and more in the next half-hour, till by eight o'clock the whole central army is gliding on. It defiles in strands by narrow tracks through the forest. Riding impatiently on the outskirts of the columns is MARSHAL NEY, who has as yet received no command.

As the day develops, sight and sounds to the left and right reveal that the two outside columns have also started, and are creeping towards the frontier abreast with the centre. That the whole forms one great movement, co-ordinated by one mind, now becomes apparent.

Preceded by scouts the three columns converge.

The advance through dense woods by narrow paths takes time. The head of the middles and main column forces back some outposts, and reaches Charleroi, driving out the Prussian general ZIETEN. It seizes the bridge over the Sambre and blows up the gates of the town.

The point of observation now descends close to the scene.

In the midst comes the EMPEROR with the Sappers of the Guard, the Marines, and the Young Guard. The clatter brings the scared inhabitants to their doors and windows. Cheers arise from some of them as NAPOLEON passes up the steep street. Just beyond the town, in front of the Bellevue Inn, he dismounts. A chair is brought out, in which he sits and surveys the whole valley of the Sambre. The troops march past cheering him, and drums roll and bugles blow. Soon the EMPEROR is found to be asleep.

When the rattle of their passing ceases the silence wakes him. His listless eye falls upon a half-defaced poster on a wall opposite—the Declaration of the Allies.

NAPOLEON [reading]
"... Bonaparte destroys the only legal title on which his existence depended.... He has deprived himself of the protection of the law, and has manifested to the Universe that there can be neither peace nor truce with him. The Powers consequently declare that Napoleon Bonaparte has placed himself without the pale of civil and social relations, and that as an enemy and disturber of the tranquility of the world he has rendered himself liable to public vengeance."

His flesh quivers, and he turns with a start, as if fancying that some one may be about to stab him in the back. Then he rises, mounts, and rides on.

Meanwhile the right column crosses the Sambre without difficulty at Chatelet, a little lower down; the left column at Marchienne a little higher up; and the three limbs combine into one vast army.

As the curtain of the mist is falling, the point of vision soars again, and there is afforded a brief glimpse of what is doing far away on the other side. From all parts of Europe long and sinister black files are crawling hitherward in serpentine lines, like slowworms through grass. They are the advancing armies of the Allies. The Dumb Show ends.

SCENE II

A BALLROOM IN BRUSSELS (3)

[It is a June midnight at the DUKE AND DUCHESS OF RICHMOND'S. A band of stringed instruments shows in the background. The room is crowded with a brilliant assemblage of more than two hundred of the distinguished people sojourning in the city on account of the war and other reasons, and of local personages of State and fashion. The ball has opened with "The White Cockade."

Among those discovered present either dancing or looking on are the DUKE and DUCHESS as host and hostess, their son and eldest daughter, the Duchess's brother, the DUKE OF WELLINGTON, the PRINCE OF ORANGE, the DUKE OF BRUNSWICK, BARON VAN CAPELLEN the Belgian Secretary of State, the DUKE OF ARENBERG, the MAYOR OF BRUSSELS, the DUKE AND DUCHESS OF BEAUFORT, GENERAL ALAVA, GENERAL OUDENARDE, LORD HILL, LORD AND LADY CONYNGHAM, SIR HENRY AND LADY SUSAN CLINTON, SIR H. AND LADY HAMILTON DALRYMPLE, SIR WILLIAM AND LADY DE LANCEY, LORD UXBRIDGE, SIR JOHN BYNG, LORD PORTARLINGTON, LORD EDWARD SOMERSET, LORD HAY, COLONEL ABERCROMBY, SIR HUSSEY VIVIAN, SIR A. GORDON, SIR W. PONSONBY, SIR DENIS PACK, SIR JAMES KEMPT, SIR THOMAS PICTON, GENERAL MAITLAND, COLONEL CAMERON, many other officers, English, Hanoverian, Dutch and Belgian ladies English and foreign, and Scotch reel-dancers from Highland regiments.

The "Hungarian Waltz" having also been danced, the hostess calls up the Highland soldiers to show the foreign guests what a Scotch reel is like. The men put their hands on their hips and tread it out briskly. While they stand aside and rest "The Hanoverian Dance" is called.

Enter LIEUTENANT WEBSTER, A.D.C. to the PRINCE OF ORANGE. The Prince goes apart with him and receives a dispatch. After reading it he speaks to WELLINGTON, and the two, accompanied by the DUKE OF RICHMOND, retire into an alcove with serious faces. WEBSTER, in passing back across the ballroom, exchanges a hasty word with two of three of the guests known to him, a young officer among them, and goes out.

YOUNG OFFICER [to partner]
The French have passed the Sambre at Charleroi!

PARTNER
What—does it mean the Bonaparte indeed
Is bearing down upon us?

YOUNG OFFICER
That is so.
The one who spoke to me in passing out
Is Aide to the Prince of Orange, bringing him
Dispatches from Rebecque, his chief of Staff,
Now at the front, not far from Braine le Comte;
He says that Ney, leading the French van-guard,
Has burst on Quatre-Bras.

PARTNER
O horrid time!
Will you, then, have to go and face him there?

YOUNG OFFICER
I shall, of course, sweet. Promptly too, no doubt.
[He gazes about the room.]
See—the news spreads; the dance is paralyzed.
They are all whispering round. [The band stops.] Here comes one more,
He's the attache from the Prussian force
At our headquarters.

[Enter GENERAL MUFFLING. He looks prepossessed, and goes straight to WELLINGTON and RICHMOND in the alcove, who by this time have been joined by the DUKE OF BRUNSWICK.]

SEVERAL GUESTS [at back of room]
Yes, you see, it's true!
The army will prepare to march at once.

PICTON [to another general]
I am damn glad we are to be off. Pottering about her pinned to petticoat tails—it does one no good, but blasted harm!

ANOTHER GUEST
The ball cannot go on, can it? Didn't the Duke know the French were so near? If he did, how could he let us run risks so coolly?

LADY HAMILTON DALRYMPLE [to partner]
A deep concern weights those responsible
Who gather in the alcove. Wellington
Affects a cheerfulness in outward port,
But cannot rout his real anxiety!

[The DUCHESS OF RICHMOND goes to her husband.]

DUCHESS
Ought I to stop the ball? It hardly seems right to let it continue if all be true.

RICHMOND

I have put that very question to Wellington, my dear. He says that we need not hurry off the guests.
The men have to assemble some time before the officers, who can stay on here a little longer without
inconvenience; and he would prefer that they should, not to create a panic in the city, where the friends
and spies of Napoleon are all agog for some such thing, which they would instantly communicate to him
to take advantage of.

DUCHESS
Is it safe to stay on? Should we not be thinking about getting the children away?

RICHMOND
There's no hurry at all, even if Bonaparte were really sure to enter. But he's never going to set foot in
Brussels—don't you imagine it for a moment.

DUCHESS [anxiously]
I hope not. But I wish we had never brought them here!

RICHMOND
It is too late, my dear, to wish that now. Don't be flurried; make the people go on dancing.

[The DUCHESS returns to her guests. The DUKE rejoins WELLINGTON, BRUNSWICK, MUFFLING, and the
PRINCE OF ORANGE in the alcove.]

WELLINGTON
We need not be astride till five o'clock
If all the men are marshalled well ahead.
The Brussels citizens must not suppose
They stand in serious peril... He, I think,
Directs his main attack mistakenly;
It should gave been through Mons, not Charleroi.

MUFFLING
The Austrian armies, and the Russian too,
Will show nowhere in this. The thing that's done,
Be it a historied feat or nine days' fizz,
Will be done long before they join us here.

WELLINGTON
Yes, faith; and 'tis pity. But, by God,
Blucher, I think, and I can make a shift
To do the business without troubling 'em!
Though I've an infamous army, that's the truth,—
Weak, and but ill-equipped,—and what's as bad,
A damned unpractised staff!

MUFFLING
We'll hope for luck.
Blucher concentrates certainly by now
Near Ligny, as he says in his dispatch.

Your Grace, I glean, will mass at Quatre-Bras?

WELLINGTON
Ay, now we are sure this move on Charleroi
Is no mere feint. Though I had meant Nivelles.
Have ye a good map, Richmond, near at hand?

RICHMOND
In the next room there's one. [Exit RICHMOND.]

[WELLINGTON calls up various general officers and aides from other parts of the room. PICTON, UXBRIDGE, HILL, CLINTON, VIVIAN, MAITLAND, PONSONBY, SOMERSET, and others join him in succession, receive orders, and go out severally.]

PRINCE OF ORANGE
As my divisions seem to lie around
The probable point of impact, it behoves me
To start at once, Duke, for Genappe, I deem?
Being in Brussels, all for this damned ball,
The dispositions out there have, so far,
Been made by young Saxe Weimar and Perponcher,
On their own judgment quite. I go, your Grace?

WELLINGTON
Yes, certainly. 'Tis now desirable.
Farewell! Good luck, until we meet again,
The battle won!

[Exit PRINCE OF ORANGE, and shortly after, MUFFLING. RICHMOND returns with a map, which he spreads out on the table. WELLINGTON scans it closely.]

Napoleon has befooled me,
By God he has,—gained four-and-twenty hours'
Good march upon me!

RICHMOND
What do you mean to do?

WELLINGTON
I have bidden the army concentrate in strength
At Quatre-Bras. But we shan't stop him there;
So I must fight him HERE.

[He marks Waterloo with his thumbnail.]

Well, now I have sped,
All necessary orders I may sup,
And then must say good-bye. [To Brunswick.] This very day

There will be fighting, Duke. You are fit to start?

BRUNSWICK [coming forward]
I leave almost this moment.—Yes, your Grace—
And I sheath not my sword till I have avenged
My father's death. I have sworn it!

WELLINGTON
My good friend,
Something too solemn knells beneath your words.
Take cheerful views of the affair in hand,
And fall to't with sang froid!

BRUNSWICK
But I have sworn!
Adieu. The rendezvous is Quatre-Bras?

WELLINGTON
Just so. The order is unchanged. Adieu;
But only till a later hour to-day;
I see it is one o'clock.

[WELLINGTON and RICHMOND go out of the alcove and join the hostess, BRUNSWICK'S black figure being left there alone. He bends over the map for a few seconds.]

SPIRIT OF THE YEARS
O Brunswick, Duke of Deathwounds! Even as he
For whom thou wear'st that filial weedery
Was waylaid by my tipstaff nine years since,
So thou this day shalt feel his fendless tap,
And join thy sire!

BRUNSWICK [starting up]
I am stirred by inner words,
As 'twere my father's angel calling me,—
That prelude to our death my lineage know!

[He stands in a reverie for a moment; then, bidding adieu to the DUCHESS OF RICHMOND and her daughter, goes slowly out of the ballroom by a side-door.]

DUCHESS
The Duke of Brunswick bore him gravely here.
His sable shape has stuck me all the eve
As one of those romantic presences
We hear of—seldom see.

WELLINGTON [phlegmatically]
Romantic,—well,

It may be so. Times often, ever since
The Late Duke's death, his mood has tinged him thus.
He is of those brave men who danger see,
And seeing front it,—not of those, less brave
But counted more, who face it sightlessly.

YOUNG OFFICER [to partner]
The Generals slip away! I, Love, must take
The cobbled highway soon. Some hours ago
The French seized Charleroi; so they loom nigh.

PARTNER [uneasily]
Which tells me that the hour you draw your sword
Looms nigh us likewise!

YOUNG OFFICER
Some are saying here
We fight this very day. Rumours all-shaped
Fly round like cockchafers!

[Suddenly there echoes in the ballroom a long-drawn metallic purl of sound, making all the company start.]

Ah—there it is,
Just as I thought! They are beating the Generale.

[The loud roll of side-drums is taken up by other drums further and further away, till the hollow noise spreads all over the city. Dismay is written on the faces of the women. The Highland non-commissioned officers and privates march smartly down the ballroom and disappear.]

SPIRIT OF THE PITIES
Discerned you stepping out in front of them
That figure—of a pale drum-major kind,
Or fugleman—who wore a cold grimace?

SPIRIT OF THE YEARS
He was my old fiend Death, in rarest trim,
The occasion favouring his husbandry!

SPIRIT OF THE PITIES
Are those who marched behind him, then, to fall?

SPIRIT OF THE YEARS
Ay, all well-nigh, ere Time have houred three-score.

PARTNER
Surely this cruel call to instant war
Spares space for one dance more, that memory

May store when you are gone, while I—sad me!—
Wait, wait and weep.... Yes—one there is to be!

SPIRIT IRONIC
Methinks flirtation grows too tender here!

[Country Dance, "The Prime of Life," a favourite figure at this period. The sense of looming tragedy
carries emotion to its climax. All the younger officers stand up with their partners, forming several
figures of fifteen or twenty couples each. The air is ecstasizing, and both sexes abandon themselves to
the movement.

Nearly half an hour passes before the figure is danced down. Smothered kisses follow the conclusion.
The silence is broken from without by more long hollow rolling notes, so near that they thrill the
window-panes.]

SEVERAL
'Tis the Assemble. Now, then, we must go!

[The officers bid farewell to their partners and begin leaving in twos and threes. When they are gone
the women mope and murmur to each other by the wall, and listen to the tramp of men and slamming
of doors in the streets without.]

LADY HAMILTON DALRYMPLE
The Duke has borne him gaily here to-night.
The youngest spirits scarcely capped his own.

DALRYMPLE
Maybe that, finding himself blade to blade
With Bonaparte at last, his blood gets quick.
French lancers of the Guard were seen at Frasnes
Last midnight; so the clash is not far off.

[They leave.]

DE LANCEY [to his wife]
I take you to our door, and say good-bye,
And go thence to the Duke's and wait for him.
In a few hours we shall be all in motion
Towards the scene of—what we cannot tell!
You, dear, will haste to Antwerp till it's past,
As we have arranged.

[They leave.]

WELLINGTON [to Richmond]
Now I must also go,
And snatch a little snooze ere harnessing.
The Prince and Brunswick have been gone some while.

[RICHMOND walks to the door with him. Exit WELLINGTON, RICHMOND returns.]

DUCHESS [to Richmond]
Some of these left renew the dance, you see.
I cannot stop them; but with memory hot
Of those late gone, of where they are gone, and why,
It smacks of heartlessness!

RICHMOND
Let be; let be;
Youth comes not twice to fleet mortality!

[The dancing, however, is fitful and spiritless, few but civilian partners being left for the ladies. Many of the latter prefer to sit in reverie while waiting for their carriages.]

SPIRIT OF THE PITIES
When those stout men-at-arms drew forward there,
I saw a like grimacing shadow march
And pirouette before no few of them.
Some of themselves beheld it; some did not.

SPIRIT OF THE YEARS
Which were so ushered?

SPIRIT OF THE PITIES
Brunswick, who saw and knew;
One also moved before Sir Thomas Picton,
Who coolly conned and drily spoke to it;
Another danced in front of Ponsonby,
Who failed of heeding his.—De Lancey, Hay,
Gordon, and Cameron, and many more
Were footmanned by like phantoms from the ball.

SPIRIT OF THE YEARS
Multiplied shimmerings of my Protean friend,
Who means to couch them shortly. Thou wilt eye
Many fantastic moulds of him ere long,
Such as, bethink thee, oft hast eyed before.

SPIRIT OF THE PITIES
I have—too often!

[The attenuated dance dies out, the remaining guests depart, the musicians leave the gallery and depart also. RICHMOND goes to a window and pulls back one of the curtains. Dawn is barely visible in the sky, and the lamps indistinctly reveal that long lines of British infantry have assembled in the street. In the irksomeness of waiting for their officers with marching-orders, they have lain down on the pavements, where many are soundly sleeping, their heads on their knapsacks and their arms by their side.]

DUCHESS
Poor men. Sleep waylays them. How tired they seem!

RICHMOND
They'll be more tired before the day is done.
A march of eighteen miles beneath the heat,
And then to fight a battle ere they rest,
Is what foreshades.—Well, it is more than bed-time;
But little sleep for us or any one
To-night in Brussels!

[He draws the window-curtain and goes out with the DUCHESS. Servants enter and extinguish candles.
The scene closes in darkness.]

SCENE III

CHARLEROI. NAPOLEON'S QUARTERS

[The same midnight. NAPOLEON is lying on a bed in his clothes. In consultation with SOULT, his Chief of
Staff, who is sitting near, he dictates to his Secretary orders for the morrow. They are addressed to
KELLERMANN, DROUOT, LOBAU, GERARD, and other of his marshals. SOULT goes out to dispatch them.

The Secretary resumes the reading of reports. Presently MARSHAL NEY is announced He is heard
stumbling up the stairs, and enters.]

NAPOLEON
Ah, Ney; why come you back? Have you secured
The all-important Crossways?—safely sconced
Yourself at Quatre-Bras?

NEY
Not, sire, as yet.
For, marching forwards, I heard gunnery boom,
And, fearing that the Prussians had engaged you,
I stood at pause. Just then—

NAPOLEON
My charge was this:
Make it impossible at any cost
That Wellington and Blucher should unite.
As it's from Brussels that the English come,
And from Namur the Prussians, Quatre-Bras
Lends it alone for their forgathering:
So, why exists it not in your hands/

NEY

My reason, sire, was rolling from my tongue.—
Hard on the boom of guns, dim files of foot
Which read to me like massing Englishry—
The vanguard of all Wellington's array—
I half-discerned. So, in pure wariness,
I left the Bachelu columns there at Frasnes,
And hastened back to tell you.

NAPOLEON

Ney; O Ney!
I fear you are not the man that once you were;
Of your so daring, such a faint-heart now!
I have ground to know the foot that flustered you
Were but a few stray groups of Netherlanders;
For my good spies in Brussels send me cue
That up to now the English have not stirred,
But cloy themselves with nightly revel there.

NEY [bitterly]

Give me another opportunity
Before you speak like that!

NAPOLEON

You soon will have one!...
But now—no more of this. I have other glooms
Upon my soul—the much-disquieting news
That Bourmont has deserted to our foes
With his whole staff.

NEY

We can afford to let him.

NAPOLEON

It is what such betokens, not their worth,
That whets it!... Love, respect for me, have waned;
But I will right that. We've good chances still.
You must return foot-hot to Quatre-Bras;
There Kellermann's cuirassiers will promptly join you
To bear the English backward Brussels way.
I go on towards Fleurus and Ligny now.—
If Blucher's force retreat, and Wellington's
Lie somnolent in Brussels one day more,
I gain that city sans a single shot!...

Now, friend, downstairs you'll find some supper ready,
Which you must tuck in sharply, and then off.
The past day has not ill-advantaged us;

We have stolen upon the two chiefs unawares,
And in such sites that they must fight apart.
Now for a two hours' rest.—Comrade, adieu
Until to-morrow!

NEY
Till to-morrow, sire!

[Exit NEY. NAPOLEON falls asleep, and the Secretary waits till dictation shall be resumed. BUSSY, the
orderly officer, comes to the door.

BUSSY
Letters—arrived from Paris. [Hands letters.]

SECRETARY
He shall have them
The moment he awakes. These eighteen hours
He's been astride; and is not what he was.—
Much news from Paris?

BUSSY
I can only say
What's not the news. The courier has just told me
He'd nothing from the Empress at Vienna
To bring his Majesty. She writes no more.

SECRETARY
And never will again! In my regard
That bird's forsook the nest for good and all.

BUSSY
All that they hear in Paris from her court
Is through our spies there. One of them reports
This rumour of her: that the Archduke John,
In taking leave to join our enemies here,
Said, "Oh, my poor Louise; I am grieved for you
And what I hope is, that he'll be run through,
Or shot, or break his neck, for your own good
No less than ours.

NAPOLEON [waking]
By "he" denoting me?

BUSSY [starting]
Just so, your Majesty.

NAPOLEON [peremptorily]
What said the Empress?

BUSSY
She gave no answer, sire, that rumour bears.

NAPOLEON
Count Neipperg, whom they have made her chamberlain,
Interred his wife last spring—is it not so?

BUSSY
He did, your Majesty.

NAPOLEON
H'm....You may go.

[Exit BUSSY. The Secretary reads letters aloud in succession. He comes to the last; begins it; reaches a phrase, and stops abruptly.]

Mind not! Read on. No doubt the usual threat,
Or prophecy, from some mad scribe? Who signs it?

SECRETARY
The subscript is "The Duke of Enghien!"

NAPOLEON [starting up]
Bah, man! A treacherous trick! A hoax—no more!
Is that the last?

SECRETARY
The last, your Majesty.

NAPOLEON
Then now I'll sleep. In two hours have me called.

SECRETARY
I'll give the order, sire.

[The Secretary goes. The candles are removed, except one, and NAPOLEON endeavours to compose himself.]

SPIRIT IRONIC
A little moral panorama would do him no harm, after that reminder of the Duke of Enghien. Shall it be, young Compassion?

SPIRIT OF THE PITIES
What good—if that old Years tells us be true?
But I say naught. To ordain is not for me!

[Thereupon a vision passes before NAPOLEON as he lies, comprising hundreds of thousands of skeletons and corpses in various stages of decay. They rise from his various battlefields, the flesh dropping from them, and gaze reproachfully at him. His intimate officers who have been slain he recognizes among the crowd. In front is the DUKE OF ENGHIEN as showman.]

NAPOLEON [in his sleep]
Why, why should this reproach be dealt me now?
Why hold me my own master, if I be
Ruled by the pitiless Planet of Destiny?

[He jumps up in a sweat and puts out the last candle; and the scene is curtained by darkness.]

SCENE IV

A CHAMBER OVERLOOKING A MAIN STREET IN BRUSSELS

[A June sunrise; the beams struggling through the window-curtains. A canopied bed in a recess on the left. The quick notes of "Brighton Camp, or the "Girl I've left behind me," strike sharply into the room from fifes and drums without. A young lady in a dressing-gown, who has evidently been awaiting the sound, springs from the bed like a hare from its form, undraws window-curtains and opens the window.

Columns of British soldiery are marching past from the Parc southward out of the city by the Namur Gate. The windows of other houses in the street rattle open, and become full of gazers.

A tap at the door. An older lady enters, and comes up to the first.]

YOUNGER LADY [turning]
O mamma—I didn't hear you!

ELDER LADY
I was sound asleep till the thumping of the drums set me fantastically dreaming, and when I awoke I found they were real. Did they wake you too, my dear?

Younger Lady [reluctantly]
I didn't require waking. I hadn't slept since we came home.

ELDER LADY
That was from the excitement of the ball. There are dark rings round your eye. [The fifes and drums are now opposite, and thrill the air in the room.] Ah—that "Girl I've left behind me!"—which so many thousands of women have throbbed an accompaniment to, and will again to-day if ever they did!

YOUNGER LADY [her voice faltering]
It is rather cruel to say that just now, mamma. There, I can't look at them after it! [She turns and wipes her eyes.]

ELDER LADY

I wasn't thinking of ourselves—certainly not of you.—How they press on—with those great knapsacks and firelocks and, I am told, fifty-six rounds of ball-cartridge, and four days' provisions in those haversacks. How can they carry it all near twenty miles and fight with it on their shoulders!... Don't cry, dear. I thought you would get sentimental last night over somebody. I ought to have brought you home sooner. How many dances did you have? It was impossible for me to look after you in the excitement of the war-tidings.

YOUNGER LADY
Only three—four.

ELDER LADY
Which were they?

YOUNGER LADY
"Enrico," the "Copenhagen Waltz" and the "Hanoverian," and the "Prime of Life."

ELDER LADY
It was very foolish to fall in love on the strength of four dances.

YOUNGER LADY [evasively]
Fall in love? Who said I had fallen in love? What a funny idea!

ELDER LADY
Is it?... Now here come the Highland Brigade with their pipes and their "Hieland Laddie." How the sweethearts cling to the men's arms. [Reaching forward.] There are more regiments following. But look, that gentleman opposite knows us. I cannot remember his name. [She bows and calls across.] Sir, which are these?

GENTLEMAN OPPOSITE
The Ninety-second. Next come the Forty-ninth, and next the Forty-second—Sir Denis Pack's brigade.

ELDER LADY
Thank you.—I think it is that gentleman we talked to at the Duchess's, but I am not sure.

[A pause: another band.]

GENTLEMAN OPPOSITE
That's the Twenty-eighth. [They pass, with their band and colours.] Now the Thirty-second are coming up—part of Kempt's brigade. Endless, are they not?

ELDER LADY
Yes, Sir. Has the Duke passed out yet?

GENTLEMAN OPPOSITE
Not yet. Some cavalry will go by first, I think. The foot coming up now are the Seventy-ninth. [They pass.]... These next are the Ninety-fifth. [They pass.]... These are the First Foot-guards now. [They pass, playing "British Grenadiers."]... The Fusileer-guards now. [They pass.] Now the Coldstreamers. [They

pass. He looks up towards the Parc.] Several Hanoverian regiments under Colonel Best are coming next. [They pass, with their bands and colours. An interval.]

ELDER LADY [to daughter]
Here are the hussars. How much more they carry to battle than at reviews. The hay in those great nets must encumber them. [She turns and sees that her daughter has become pale.] Ah, now I know! HE has just gone by. You exchanged signals with him, you wicked girl! How do you know what his character is, or if he'll ever come back?

[The younger lady goes and flings herself on her face upon the bed, sobbing silently. Her mother glances at her, but leaves her alone. An interval. The prancing of a group of horsemen is heard on the cobble-stones without.]

GENTLEMAN OPPOSITE [calling]
Here comes the Duke!

ELDER LADY [to younger]
You have left the window at the most important time! The Duke of
Wellington and his staff-officers are passing out.

YOUNGER LADY
I don't want to see him. I don't want to see anything any more!

[Riding down the street comes WELLINGTON in a grey frock-coat and small cocked hat, frigid and undemonstrative; accompanied by four or five Generals of his suite, the Deputy Quartermaster-general De LANCEY, LORD FITZROY SOMERSET, Aide-de-camp, and GENERAL MUFFLING.]

GENTLEMAN OPPOSITE
He is the Prussian officer attached to our headquarters, through whom Wellington communicates with Blucher, who, they say, is threatened by the French at Ligny at this moment.

[The elder lady turns to her daughter, and going to the bed bends over her, while the horses' tramp of WELLINGTON and his staff clatters more faintly in the street, and the music of the last retreating band dies away towards the Forest of Soignes.

Finding her daughter is hysterical with grief she quickly draws the window-curtains to screen the room from the houses opposite.

Scene ends.]

SCENE V

THE FIELD OF LIGNY

[The same day later. A prospect of the battlefield of Ligny southward from the roof of the windmill of Bussy, which stands at the centre and highest point of the Prussian position, about six miles south-east of Quatre-Bras.

The ground slopes downward along the whole front of the scene to a valley through which wanders the Ligne, a muddy stream bordered by sallows. On both sides of the stream, in the middle plane of the picture, stands the village of Ligny, composed of thatched cottages, gardens, and farm-houses with stone walls; the main features, such as the church, church-yard, and village-green being on the further side of the Ligne.

On that side the land reascends in green wheatfields to an elevation somewhat greater than that of the foreground, reaching away to Fleurus in the right-hand distance.

In front, on the slopes between the spectator and the village, is the First Corps of the Prussian army commanded by Zieten, its First Brigade under STEINMETZ occupying the most salient point.

The Corps under THIELMANN is ranged to the left, and that of PIRCH to the rear, in reserve to ZIETEN. In the centre-front, just under the mill, BLUCHER on a fine grey charger is intently watching, with his staff.

Something dark is seen to be advancing over the horizon by Fleurus, about three miles off. It is the van of NAPOLEON'S army, approaching to give battle.

At this moment hoofs are heard clattering along a road that passes behind the mill; and there come round to the front the DUKE OF WELLINGTON, his staff-officers, and a small escort of cavalry.

WELLINGTON and BLUCHER greet each other at the foot of the windmill. They disappear inside, and can be heard ascending the ladders.

Enter on the roof WELLINGTON and BLUCHER, followed by FITZROY SOMERSET, GNEISENAU, MUFFLING, and others. Before renewing their conversation they peer through their glasses at the dark movements on the horizon. WELLINGTON'S manner is deliberate, judicial, almost indifferent; BLUCHER'S eager and impetuous.

WELLINGTON
They muster not as yet in near such strength
At Quatre-Bras as here.

BLUCHER
'Tis from Fleurus
They come debouching. I, perforce, withdrew
My forward posts of cavalry at dawn
In face of their light cannon.... They'll be here
I reckon, soon!

WELLINGTON [still with glass]
I clearly see his staff,
And if my eyes don't lie, the Arch-one too....
It is the whole Imperial army, Prince,

That we've before us. [A silence.] Well, we'll cope with them!
What would you have me do?

[BLUCHER is so absorbed in what he sees that he does not heed.]

GNEISENAU
Duke, this I'd say:
Events suggest to us that you come up
With all your force, behind the village here,
And act as our reserve.

MUFFLING
But Bonaparte,
Pray note, has redistributed his strength
In fashion that you fail to recognize.
I am against your scheme.

BLUCHER [lowering his glass]
Signs notify
Napoleon's plans as changed! He purports now
To strike our left—between Sombreffe and Brye....
If so, I have to readjust my ward.

WELLINGTON
One of his two divisions that we scan
Outspreading from Fleurus, seems bent on Ligny,
The other on Saint-Amand.

BLUCHER
Well, I shall see
In half an hour, your Grace. If what I deem
Be what he means, Von Zieten's corps forthwith
Must stand to their positions: Pirch out here,
Henckel at Ligny, Steinmetz at La Haye.

WELLINGTON
So that, your Excellency, as I opine,
I go and sling my strength on their left wing—
Manoeuvring to outflank 'em on that side.

BLUCHER
True, true. Our plan uncovers of itself;
You bear down everything from Quatre-Bras
Along the road to Frasnes.

WELLINGTON
I will, by God.
I'll bear straight on to Gosselies, if needs!

GNEISENAU
Your Excellencies, if I may be a judge,
Such movement will not tend to unity;
It leans too largely on a peradventure
Most speculative in its contingencies!

[A silence; till the officers of the staff remark to each other that concentration is best in any
circumstances. A general discussion ensues.]

BLUCHER [concludingly]
We will expect you, Duke, to our support.

WELLINGTON
I must agree that, in the sum, it's best.
So be it then. If not attacked myself
I'll come to you.—Now I return with speed
To Quatre-Bras.

BLUCHER
And I descend from here
To give close eye and thought to things below;
No more can well be studied where we stand.

[Exeunt from roof WELLINGTON, BLUCHER and the rest. They reappear below, and WELLINGTON and
his suite gallop furiously away in the direction of Quatre-Bras. An interval.]

DUMB SHOW [below]
Three reports of a cannon give the signal for the French attack. NAPOLEON'S army advances down the
slopes of green corn opposite, bands and voices joining in songs of victory. The French come in three
grand columns; VANDAMME'S on the left [the spectator's right] against Saint-Amand, the most forward
angle of the Prussian position. GERARD'S in the centre bear down upon Ligny. GROUCHY'S on the
French right is further back. Far to the rear can be discerned NAPOLEON, the Imperial Guard, and
MILHAUD'S cuirassiers halted in reserve.

This formidable advance is preceded by swarms of tirailleurs, who tread down the high wheat, exposing
their own men in the rear.

Amid cannonading from both sides they draw nearer to the Prussians, though lanes are cut through
them by the latter's guns. They drive the Prussians out of Ligny; who, however, rally in the houses,
churchyard, and village green.

SPIRIT OF THE PITIES
I see unnatural an Monster, loosely jointed,
With an Apocalyptic Being's shape,
And limbs and eyes a hundred thousand strong,
And fifty thousand heads; which coils itself
About the buildings there.

SPIRIT OF THE YEARS
Thou dost indeed.
It is the Monster Devastation. Watch.

Round the church they fight without quarter, shooting face to face, stabbing with unfixed bayonets, and braining with the butts of muskets. The village catches fire, and soon becomes a furnace.

The crash of splitting timbers as doors are broken through, the curses of the fighters, rise into the air, with shouts of "En avant!" from the further side of the stream, and "Vorwarts!" from the nearer.

The battle extends to the west by Le Hameau and Saint-Amand la Haye; and Ligny becomes invisible under a shroud of smoke.

VOICES [at the base of the mill]
This sun will go down bloodily for us!
The English, sharply sighed for by Prince Blucher,
Cannot appear. Wellington words across
That hosts have set on him at Quatre-Bras,
And leave him not one bayonet to spare!

The truth of this intelligence is apparent. A low dull sound heard lately from the direction of Quatre-Bras has increased to a roaring cannonade. The scene abruptly closes.

SCENE VI

THE FIELD AT QUATRE-BRAS

[The same day. The view is southward, and the straight gaunt highway from Brussels [behind the spectator] to Charleroi over the hills in front, bisects the picture from foreground to distance. Near at hand, where it is elevated and open, there crosses it obliquely, at a point called Les Quatre-Bras, another road which comes from Nivelle, five miles to the gazer's right rear, and goes to Namur, twenty miles ahead to the left. At a distance of five or six miles in this latter direction it passes near the previous scene, Ligny, whence the booming of guns can be continuously heard.

Between the cross-roads in the centre of the scene and the far horizon the ground dips into a hollow, on the other side of which the same straight road to Charleroi is seen climbing the crest, and over it till out of sight. From a hill on the right hand of the mid-distance a large wood, the wood of Bossu, reaches up nearly to the crossways, which give their name to the buildings thereat, consisting of a few farm-houses and an inn.

About three-quarters of a mile off, nearly hidden by the horizon towards Charleroi, there is also a farmstead, Gemioncourt; another, Piraumont, stands on an eminence a mile to the left of it, and somewhat in front of the Namur road.]

DUMB SHOW

As this scene uncovers the battle is beheld to be raging at its height, and to have reached a keenly tragic phase. WELLINGTON has returned from Ligny, and the main British and Hanoverian position, held by the men who marched out of Brussels in the morning, under officers who danced the previous night at the Duchess's, is along the Namur road to the left of the perspective, and round the cross-road itself. That of the French, under Ney, is on the crests further back, from which they are descending in imposing numbers. Some advanced columns are assailing the English left, while through the smoke-hazes of the middle of the field two lines of skirmishers are seen firing at each other—the southernmost dark blue, the northernmost dull red. Time lapses till it is past four o'clock.

SPIRIT OF RUMOUR
The cannonade of the French ordnance-lines
Has now redoubled. Columns new and dense
Of foot, supported by fleet cavalry,
Straightly impinge upon the Brunswick bands
That border the plantation of Bossu.
Above some regiments of the assaulting French
A flag like midnight swims upon the air,
To say no quarter may be looked for there!

The Brunswick soldiery, much notched and torn by the French grape-shot, now lie in heaps. The DUKE OF BRUNSWICK himself, desperate to keep them steady, lights his pipe, and rides slowly up and down in front of his lines previous to the charge which follows.

SPIRIT OF RUMOUR
The French have heaved them on the Brunswickers,
And borne them back. Now comes the Duke's told time.
He gallops at the head of his hussars—
Those men of solemn and appalling guise,
Full-clothed in black, with nodding hearsy plumes,
A shining silver skull and cross of bones
Set upon each, to byspeak his slain sire....
Concordantly, the expected bullet starts
And finds the living son.

BRUNSWICK reels to the ground. His troops, disheartened, lose their courage and give way.

The French front columns, and the cavalry supporting them, shout as they advance. The Allies are forced back upon the English main position. WELLINGTON is in personal peril for a time, but he escapes it by a leap of his horse.

A curtain of smoke drops. An interval. The curtain reascends.

SPIRIT OF THE PITIES
Behold again the Dynasts' gory gear!
Since we regarded, what has progressed here?

RECORDING ANGEL [in recitative]
Musters of English foot and their allies

Came palely panting by the Brussels way,
And, swiftly stationed, checked their counter-braves.
Ney, vexed by lack of like auxiliaries,
Bade then the columned cuirassiers to charge
In all their edged array of weaponcraft.
Yea; thrust replied to thrust, and fire to fire;
The English broke, till Picton prompt to prop them
Sprang with fresh foot-folk from the covering rye.

Next, Pire's cavalry took up the charge....
And so the action sways. The English left
Is turned at Piraumont; whilst on their right
Perils infest the greenwood of Bossu;
Wellington gazes round with dubious view;
England's long fame in fight seems sepulchered,
And ominous roars swell loudlier Ligny-ward.

SPIRIT OF RUMOUR
New rage has wrenched the battle since thou'st writ;
Hot-hasting succours of light cannonry
Lately come up, relieve the English stress;
Kellermann's cuirassiers, both man and horse
All plated over with the brass of war,
Are rolling on the highway. More brigades
Of British, soiled and sweltering, now are nigh,
Who plunge within the boscage of Bossu;
Where in the hidden shades and sinuous creeps
Life-struggles can be heard, seen but in peeps.
Therewith the foe's accessions harass Ney,
Racked that no needful d'Erlon darks the way!

Inch by inch NEY has to draw off: WELLINGTON promptly advances. At dusk NEY'S army finds itself back at Frasnes, where he meets D'ERLON coming up to his assistance, too late.

The weary English and their allies, who have been on foot ever since one o'clock the previous morning, prepare to bivouac in front of the cross-roads. Their fires flash up for a while; and by and by the dead silence of heavy sleep hangs over them. WELLINGTON goes into his tent, and the night darkens.

A Prussian courier from Ligny enters, who is conducted into the tent to WELLINGTON.

SPIRIT OF THE PITIES
What tidings can a courier bring that count
Here, where such mighty things are native born?

RECORDING ANGEL [in recitative]
The fury of the tumult there begun
Scourged quivering Ligny through the afternoon:
Napoleon's great intent grew substantive,

And on the Prussian pith and pulse he bent
His foretimed blow. Blucher, to butt the shock,
Called up his last reserves, and heading on,
With blade high brandished by his aged arm,
Spurred forward his white steed. But they, outspent,
Failed far to follow. Darkness coped the sky,
And storm, and rain with thunder. Yet once more
He cheered them on to charge. His horse, the while,
Pierced by a bullet, fell on him it bore.
He, trampled, bruised, faint, and in disarray
Dragged to another mount, was led away.
His ragged lines withdraw from sight and sound,
And their assailants camp upon the ground.

The scene shuts with midnight.

SCENE VII

BRUSSELS. THE PLACE ROYALE

[The same night, dark and sultry. A crowd of citizens throng the broad Place. They gaze continually down the Rue de Namur, along which arrive minute by minute carts and waggons laden with wounded men. Other wounded limp into the city on foot. At much greater speed enter fugitive soldiers from the miscellaneous contingents of WELLINGTON'S army at Quatre-Bras, who gesticulate and explain to the crowd that all is lost and that the French will soon be in Brussels.

Baggage-carts and carriages, with and without horses, stand before an hotel, surrounded by a medley of English and other foreign nobility and gentry with their valets and maids. Bulletins from the battlefield are affixed on the corner of the Place, and people peer at them by the dim oil lights.

A rattle of hoofs reaches the ears, entering the town by the same Namur gate. The riders disclose themselves to be Belgian hussars, also from the field.]

SEVERAL HUSSARS
The French approach! Wellington is beaten. Bonaparte is at our heels.

[Consternation reaches a climax. Horses are hastily put-to at the hotel: people crowd into the carriages and try to drive off. They get jammed together and hemmed in by the throng. Unable to move they quarrel and curse despairingly in sundry tongues.]

BARON CAPELLEN
Affix the new bulletin. It is a more assuring one, and may quiet them a little.

[A new bulletin is nailed over the old one.]

MAYOR

Good people, calm yourselves. No victory has been won by Bonaparte. The noise of guns heard all the afternoon became fainter towards the end, showing beyond doubt that the retreat was away from the city.

A CITIZEN
The French are said to be forty thousand strong at Les Quatre-Bras, and no forty thousand British marched out against them this morning!

ANOTHER CITIZEN
And it is whispered that the city archives and the treasure-chest have been sent to Antwerp!

MAYOR
Only as a precaution. No good can be gained by panic. Sixty or seventy thousand of the Allies, all told, face Napoleon at this hour. Meanwhile who is to attend to the wounded that are being brought in faster and faster? Fellow-citizens, do your duty by these unfortunates, and believe me that when engaged in such an act of mercy no enemy will hurt you.

CITIZENS
What can we do?

MAYOR
I invite all those who have such, to bring mattresses, sheets, and coverlets to the Hotel de Ville, also old linen and lint from the houses of the cures.

[Many set out on this errand. An interval. Enter a courier, who speaks to the MAYOR and the BARON CAPELLEN.]

BARON CAPELLEN [to Mayor]
Better inform them immediately, to prevent a panic.

MAYOR [to Citizens]
I grieve to tell you that the Duke of Brunswick, whom you saw ride out this morning, was killed this afternoon at Les Quatre-Bras. A musket-ball passed through his bridle-hand and entered his belly. His body is now arriving. Carry yourselves gravely.

[A lane is formed in the crowd in the direction of the Rue de Namur; they wait. Presently an extemporized funeral procession, with the body of the DUKE on a gun-carriage, and a small escort of Brunswickers with carbines reversed, comes slowly up the street, their silver death's-heads shining in the lamplight. The agitation of the citizens settles into a silent gloom as the mournful train passes.]

MAYOR [to Baron Capellen]
I noticed the strange look of prepossession on his face at the ball last night, as if he knew what was going to be.

BARON CAPELLEN
The Duchess mentioned it to me.... He hated the French, if any man ever did, and so did his father before him! Here comes the English Colonel Hamilton, straight from the field. He will give us trustworthy particulars.

[Enter COLONEL HAMILTON by the Rue de Namur. He converses with the MAYOR and the BARON on the issue of the struggle.]

MAYOR
Now I will go the Hotel de Ville, and get it ready for those wounded who can find no room in private houses.

[Exeunt MAYOR, CAPELLEN, D'URSEL, HAMILTON, etc. severally. Many citizens descend in the direction of the Hotel de Ville to assist. Those who remain silently watch the carts bringing in the wounded till a late hour. The doors of houses in the Place and elsewhere are kept open, and the rooms within lighted, in expectation of more arrivals from the field. A courier gallops up, who is accosted by idlers.]

COURIER [hastily]
The Prussians are defeated at Ligny by Napoleon in person. He will be here to-morrow.

[Exit courier.]

FIRST IDLER
The devil! Then I am for welcoming him. No Antwerp for me!

OTHER IDLERS [sotto voce]
Vive l'Empereur!

[A warm summer fog from the Lower Town covers the Parc and the Place Royale.]

SCENE VIII

THE ROAD TO WATERLOO

[The view is now from Quatre-Bras backward along the road by which the English arrived. Diminishing in a straight line from the foreground to the centre of the distance it passes over Mont Saint-Jean and through Waterloo to Brussels.

It is now tinged by a moving mass of English and Allied infantry, in retreat to a new position at Mont Saint-Jean. The sun shines brilliantly upon the foreground as yet, but towards Waterloo and the Forest of Soignes on the north horizon it is overcast with black clouds which are steadily advancing up the sky.

To mask the retreat the English outposts retain their position on the battlefield in the face of NEY'S troops, and keep up a desultory firing: the cavalry for the same reason remain, being drawn up in lines beside the intersecting Namur road.

Enter WELLINGTON, UXBRIDGE [who is in charge of the cavalry], MUFFLING, VIVIAN, and others. They look through their field-glasses towards Frasnes, NEY'S position since his retreat yesternight, and also towards NAPOLEON'S at Ligny.]

WELLINGTON
The noonday sun, striking so strongly there,
Makes mirrors of their arms. That they advance
Their glowing radiance shows. Those gleams by Marbais
Suggest fixed bayonets.

UXBRIDGE
Vivian's glass reveals
That they are cuirassiers. Ney's troops, too, near
At last, methinks, along this other road.

WELLINGTON
One thing is sure: that here the whole French force
Schemes to unite and sharply follow us.
It formulates our fence. The cavalry
Must linger here no longer; but recede
To Mont Saint-Jean, as rearguard of the foot.
From the intelligence that Gordon brings
'Tis pretty clear old Blucher had to take
A damned good drubbing yesterday at Ligny,
And has been bent hard back! So that, for us,
Bound to the plighted plan, there is no choice
But do like.... No doubt they'll say at home
That we've been well thrashed too. It can't be helped,
They must!... [He looks round at the sky.] A heavy rainfall threatens us,
To make it all the worse!

[The speaker and his staff ride off along the Brussels road in the rear of the infantry, and UXBRIDGE
begins the retreat of the cavalry. CAPTAIN MERCER enters with a light battery.]

MERCER [excitedly]
Look back, my lord;
Is it not Bonaparte himself we see
Upon the road I have come by?

UXBRIDGE [looking through glass]
Yes, by God;
His face as clear-cut as the edge of a cloud
The sun behind shows up! His suite and all!
Fire—fire! And aim you well.

[The battery makes ready and fires.]

No! It won't do.
He brings on mounted ordnance of his Guard,
So we're in danger here. Then limber up,
And off as soon as may be.

[The English artillery and cavalry retreat at full speed, just as the weather bursts, with flashes of lightning and drops of rain. They all clatter off along the Brussels road, UXBRIDGE and his aides galloping beside the column; till no British are left at Quatre-Bras except the slain.

The focus of the scene follows the retreating English army, the highway and its and margins panoramically gliding past the vision of the spectator. The phantoms chant monotonously while the retreat goes on.]

CHORUS OF RUMOURS [aerial music]
Day's nether hours advance; storm supervenes
In heaviness unparalleled, that screens
With water-woven gauzes, vapour-bred,
The creeping clumps of half-obliterate red—
Severely harassed past each round and ridge
By the inimical lance. They gain the bridge
And village of Genappe, in equal fence
With weather and the enemy's violence.
—Cannon upon the foul and flooded road,
Cavalry in the cornfields mire-bestrowed,
With frothy horses floundering to their knees,
Make wayfaring a moil of miseries!
Till Britishry and Bonapartists lose
Their clashing colours for the tawny hues
That twilight sets on all its stealing tinct imbues.

[The rising ground of Mont Saint-Jean, in front of Waterloo, is gained by the English vanguard and main masses of foot, and by degrees they are joined by the cavalry and artillery. The French are but little later in taking up their position amid the cornfields around La Belle Alliance.

Fires begin to shine up from the English bivouacs. Camp kettles are slung, and the men pile arms and stand round the blaze to dry themselves. The French opposite lie down like dead men in the dripping green wheat and rye, without supper and without fire.

By and by the English army also lies down, the men huddling together on the ploughed mud in their wet blankets, while some sleep sitting round the dying fires.]

CHORUS OF THE YEARS [aerial music]
The eyelids of eve fall together at last,
And the forms so foreign to field and tree
Lie down as though native, and slumber fast!

CHORUS OF THE PITIES
Sore are the thrills of misgiving we see
In the artless champaign at this harlequinade,
Distracting a vigil where calm should be!

The green seems opprest, and the Plain afraid
Of a Something to come, whereof these are the proofs,—

Neither earthquake, nor storm, nor eclipses's shade!

CHORUS OF THE YEARS
Yea, the coneys are scared by the thud of hoofs,
And their white scuts flash at their vanishing heels,
And swallows abandon the hamlet-roofs.

The mole's tunnelled chambers are crushed by wheels,
The lark's eggs scattered, their owners fled;
And the hedgehog's household the sapper unseals.

The snail draws in at the terrible tread,
But in vain; he is crushed by the felloe-rim
The worm asks what can be overhead,

And wriggles deep from a scene so grim,
And guesses him safe; for he does not know
What a foul red flood will be soaking him!

Beaten about by the heel and toe
Are butterflies, sick of the day's long rheum,
To die of a worse than the weather-foe.

Trodden and bruised to a miry tomb
Are ears that have greened but will never be gold,
And flowers in the bud that will never bloom.

CHORUS OF THE PITIES
So the season's intent, ere its fruit unfold,
Is frustrate, and mangled, and made succumb,
Like a youth of promise struck stark and cold!...

And what of these who to-night have come?

CHORUS OF THE YEARS
The young sleep sound; but the weather awakes
In the veterans, pains from the past that numb;

Old stabs of Ind, old Peninsular aches,
Old Friedland chills, haunt their moist mud bed,
Cramps from Austerlitz; till their slumber breaks.

CHORUS OF SINISTER SPIRITS
And each soul shivers as sinks his head
On the loam he's to lease with the other dead
From to-morrow's mist-fall till Time be sped!

[The fires of the English go out, and silence prevails, save for the soft hiss of the rain that falls impartially on both the sleeping armies.]

ACT SEVENTH

SCENE I

THE FIELD OF WATERLOO

[An aerial view of the battlefield at the time of sunrise is disclosed.

The sky is still overcast, and rain still falls. A green expanse, almost unbroken, of rye, wheat, and clover, in oblong and irregular patches undivided by fences, covers the undulating ground, which sinks into a shallow valley between the French and English positions. The road from Brussels to Charleroi runs like a spit through both positions, passing at the back of the English into the leafy forest of Soignes.

The latter are turning out from their bivouacs. They move stiffly from their wet rest, and hurry to and fro like ants in an ant-hill. The tens of thousands of moving specks are largely of a brick-red colour, but the foreign contingent is darker.

Breakfasts are cooked over smoky fires of green wood. Innumerable groups, many in their shirt-sleeves, clean their rusty firelocks, drawing or exploding the charges, scrape the mud from themselves, and pipeclay from their cross-belts the red dye washed off their jackets by the rain.

At six o'clock, they parade, spread out, and take up their positions in the line of battle, the front of which extends in a wavy riband three miles long, with three projecting bunches at Hougomont, La Haye Sainte, and La Haye.

Looking across to the French positions we observe that after advancing in dark streams from where they have passed the night they, too, deploy and wheel into their fighting places—figures with red epaulettes and hairy knapsacks, their arms glittering like a display of cutlery at a hill-side fair.

They assume three concentric lines of crescent shape, that converge on the English midst, with great blocks of the Imperial Guard at the back of them. The rattle of their drums, their fanfarades, and their bands playing "Veillons au salut de l'Empire" contrast with the quiet reigning on the English side.

A knot of figures, comprising WELLINGTON with a suite of general and other staff-officers, ride backwards and forwards in front of the English lines, where each regimental colour floats in the hands of the junior ensign. The DUKE himself, now a man of forty-six, is on his bay charger Copenhagen, in light pantaloons, a small plumeless hat, and a blue cloak, which shows its white lining when blown back.

On the French side, too, a detached group creeps along the front in preliminary survey. BONAPARTE—also forty-six—in a grey overcoat, is mounted on his white arab Marengo, and accompanied by SOULT, NEY, JEROME, DROUOT, and other marshals. The figures of aides move to and fro like shuttle-cocks between the group and distant points in the field. The sun has begun to gleam.]

SPIRIT OF THE PITIES
Discriminate these, and what they are,
Who stand so stalwartly to war.

SPIRIT OF THE YEARS
Report, ye Rumourers of things near and far.

SEMICHORUS I OF RUMOURS [chanting]
Sweep first the Frenchmen's leftward lines along,
And eye the peaceful panes of Hougomont—
That seemed to hold prescriptive right of peace
In fee from Time till Time itself should cease!—
Jarred now by Reille's fierce foot-divisions three,
Flanked on their left by Pire's cavalry.—
The fourfold corps of d'Erlon, spread at length,
Compose the right, east of the famed chaussee—
The shelterless Charleroi-and-Brussels way,—
And Jacquinot's alert light-steeded strength
Still further right, their sharpened swords display.
Thus stands the first line.

SEMICHORUS II
Next behind its back
Comes Count Lobau, left of the Brussels track;
Then Domon's horse, the horse of Subervie;
Kellermann's cuirassed troopers twinkle-tipt,
And, backing d'Erlon, Milhaud's horse, equipt
Likewise in burnished steelwork sunshine-dipt:
So ranks the second line refulgently.

SEMICHORUS I
The third and last embattlement reveals
D'Erlon's, Lobau's, and Reille's foot-cannoniers,
And horse-drawn ordnance too, on massy wheels,
To strike with cavalry where space appears.

SEMICHORUS II
The English front, to left, as flanking force,
Has Vandeleur's hussars, and Vivian's horse;
Next them pace Picton's rows along the crest;
The Hanoverian foot-folk; Wincke; Best;
Bylandt's brigade, set forward fencelessly,
Pack's northern clansmen, Kempt's tough infantry,
With gaiter, epaulet, spat, and {philibeg};
While Halkett, Ompteda, and Kielmansegge
Prolong the musters, near whose forward edge
Baring invests the Farm of Holy Hedge.

SEMICHORUS I

Maitland and Byng in Cooke's division range,
And round dun Hougomont's old lichened sides
A dense array of watching Guardsmen hides
Amid the peaceful produce of the grange,
Whose new-kerned apples, hairy gooseberries green,
And mint, and thyme, the ranks intrude between.—
Last, westward of the road that finds Nivelles,
Duplat draws up, and Adam parallel.

SEMICHORUS II

The second British line—embattled horse—
Holds the reverse slopes, screened, in ordered course;
Dornberg's, and Arentsschildt's, and Colquhoun-Grant's,
And left of them, behind where Alten plants
His regiments, come the "Household" Cavalry;
And nigh, in Picton's rear, the trumpets call
The "Union" brigade of Ponsonby.
Behind these the reserves. In front of all,
Or interspaced, with slow-matched gunners manned,
Upthroated rows of threatful ordnance stand.

[The clock of Nivelles convent church strikes eleven in the distance. Shortly after, coils of starch-blue smoke burst into being along the French lines, and the English batteries respond promptly, in an ominous roar that can be heard at Antwerp.

A column from the French left, six thousand strong, advances on the plantation in front of the chateau of Hougomont. They are played upon by the English ordnance; but they enter the wood, and dislodge some battalions there. The French approach the buildings, but are stopped by a loop-holed wall with a mass of English guards behind it. A deadly fire bursts from these through the loops and over the summit.

NAPOLEON orders a battery of howitzers to play upon the building.

Flames soon burst from it; but the foot-guards still hold the courtyard.]

SCENE II

THE SAME. THE FRENCH POSITION

[On a hillock near the farm of Rossomme a small table from the farmhouse has been placed; maps are spread thereon, and a chair is beside it. NAPOLEON, SOULT, and other marshals are standing round, their horses waiting at the base of the slope.

NAPOLEON looks through his glass at Hougomont. His elevated face makes itself distinct in the morning light as a gloomy resentful countenance, blue-black where shaven, and stained with snuff, with powderings of the same on the breast of his uniform. His stumpy figure, being just now thrown back, accentuates his stoutness.]

NAPOLEON
Let Reille be warned that these his surly sets
On Hougomont chateau, can scarce defray
Their mounting bill of blood. They do not touch
The core of my intent—to pierce and roll
The centre upon the right of those opposed.
Thereon will turn the outcome of the day,
In which our odds are ninety to their ten!

SOULT
Yes—prove there time and promptitude enough
To call back Grouchy here. Of his approach
I see no sign.

NAPOLEON [roughly]
Hours past he was bid come.
—But naught imports it! We are enough without him.
You have been beaten by this Wellington,
And so you think him great. But let me teach you
Wellington is no foe to reckon with.
His army, too, is poor. This clash to-day
Is more serious for our seasoned files
Than breakfasting.

SOULT
Such is my earnest hope.

NAPOLEON
Observe that Wellington still labours on,
Stoutening his right behind Gomont chateau,
But leaves his left and centre as before—
Weaker, if anything. He plays our game!

[WELLINGTON can, in fact, be seen detaching from his main line several companies of Guards to check the aims of the French on Hougomont.]

Let me re-word my tactics. Ney leads off
By seizing Mont Saint-Jean. Then d'Erlon stirs,
And heaves up his division from the left.
The second corps will move abreast of him
The sappers nearing to entrench themselves
Within the aforesaid farm.

[Enter an aide-de-camp.]

AIDE
From Marshal Ney,
Sire, I bring hasty word that all is poised
To strike the vital stroke, and only waits
Your Majesty's command,

NAPOLEON
Which he shall have
When I have scanned the hills for Grouchy's helms.

[NAPOLEON turns his glass to an upland four or five miles off on the right, known as St. Lambert's Chapel Hill. Gazing more and more intently, he takes rapid pinches of snuff in excitement.

NEY'S columns meanwhile standing for the word to advance, eighty guns being ranged in front of La Belle Alliance in support of them.]

I see a darkly crawling, slug-like shape
Embodying far out there,—troops seemingly—
Grouchy's van-guard. What think you?

SOULT [also examining closely]
Verily troops;
And, maybe, Grouchy's. But the air is hazed.

NAPOLEON
If troops at all, they are Grouchy's. Why misgive,
And force on ills you fear!

ANOTHER MARSHAL
It seems a wood.
Trees don bold outlines in their new-leafed pride.

ANOTHER MARSHAL
It is the creeping shadow from a cloud.

ANOTHER MARSHAL
It is a mass of stationary foot;
I can descry piled arms.

[NAPOLEON sends off the order for NEY'S attack—the grand assault on the English midst, including the farm of La Haye Sainte. It opens with a half-hour's thunderous discharge of artillery, which ceases at length to let d'Erlon's infantry pass.

Four huge columns of these, shouting defiantly, push forwards in face of the reciprocal fire from the cannon of the English. Their effrontery carries them so near the Anglo-Allied lines that the latter waver.

But PICTON brings up PACK'S brigade, before which the French in turn recede, though they make an attempt in La Haye Sainte, whence BARING'S Germans pour a resolute fire.

WELLINGTON, who is seen afar as one of a group standing by a great elm, orders OMPTEDA to send assistance to BARING, as may be gathered from the darting of aides to and fro between the points, like house-flies dancing their quadrilles.

East of the great highway the right columns of D'ERLON'S corps have climbed the slopes. BYLANDT'S sorely exposed Dutch are broken, and in their flight disorder the ranks of the English Twenty-eighth, the Carabineers of the Ninety-fifth being also dislodged from the sand-pit they occupied.]

NAPOLEON
All prospers marvellously! Gomont is hemmed;
La Haye Sainte too; their centre jeopardized;
Travers and d'Erlon dominate the crest,
And further strength of foot is following close.
Their troops are raw; the flower of England's force
That fought in Spain, America now holds.—

[SIR TOMAS PICTON, seeing what is happening orders KEMPT'S brigade forward. It volleys murderously DONZELOT'S columns of D'ERLON'S corps, and repulses them. As they recede PICTON is beheld shouting an order to charge.]

SPIRIT OF RUMOUR
I catch a voice that cautions Picton now
Against his rashness. "What the hell care I,—
Is my curst carcase worth a moment's mind?—
Come on!" he answers. Onwardly he goes!

[His tall, stern, saturnine figure with its bronzed complexion is on nearer approach discerned heading the charge. As he advances to the slope between the cross-roads and the sand-pit, riding very conspicuously, he falls dead, a bullet in his forehead. His aide, assisted by a soldier, drags the body beneath a tree and hastens on. KEMPT takes his command.

Next MARCOGNET is repulsed by PACK'S brigade. D'ERLON'S infantry and TRAVERS'S cuirassiers are charged by the Union Brigade of Scotch (4) Greys, Royal Dragoons, and Inniskillens, and cut down everywhere, the brigade following them so furiously the LORD UXBRIDGE tries in vain to recall it. On its coming near the French it is overwhelmed by MILHAUD'S cuirassiers, scarcely a fifth of the brigade returning.

An aide enters to NAPOLEON from GENERAL DOMON.]

AIDE
The General, on a far reconnaissance,
Says, sire, there is no room for longer doubt
That those debouching on St. Lambert's Hill
Are Prussian files.

NAPOLEON
Then where is General Grouchy?

[Enter COLONEL MARBOT with a prisoner.]

Aha—a Prussian, too! How comes he here?

MARBOT
Sire, my hussars have captured him near Lasnes—
A subaltern of the Silesian Horse.
A note from Bulow to Lord Wellington,
Announcing that a Prussian corps is close,
Was found on him. He speaks our language, sire.

NAPOLEON [to prisoner]
What force looms yonder on St. Lambert's Hill?

PRISONER
General Count Bulow's van, your Majesty.

[A thoughtful scowl crosses NAPOLEONS'S sallow face.]

NAPOLEON
Where, then, did your main army lie last night?

PRISONER
At Wavre.

NAPOLEON
But clashed it with no Frenchmen there?

PRISONER
With none. We deemed they had marched on Plancenoit.

NAPOLEON [shortly]
Take him away. [The prisoner is removed.] Has Grouchy's whereabouts
Been sought, to apprize him of this Prussian trend?

SOULT
Certainly, sire. I sent a messenger.

NAPOLEON [bitterly]
A messenger! Had my poor Berthier been here
Six would have insufficed! Now then: seek Ney;
Bid him to sling the valour of his braves
Fiercely on England ere Count Bulow come;
And advertize the succours on the hill
As Grouchy's. [Aside] This is my one battle-chance;

The Allies have many such! [To SOULT] If Bulow nears,
He cannot join in time to share the fight.
And if he could, 'tis but a corps the more....
This morning we had ninety chances ours,
We have threescore still. If Grouchy but retrieve
His fault of absence, conquest comes with eve!

[The scene shifts.]

SCENE III

SAINT LAMBERT'S CHAPEL HILL

[A hill half-way between Wavre and the fields of Waterloo, five miles to the north-east of the scene preceding. The hill is wooded, with some open land around. To the left of the scene, towards Waterloo, is a valley.]

DUMB SHOW
Marching columns in Prussian uniforms, coming from the direction of Wavre, debouch upon the hill from the road through the wood.

They are the advance-guard and two brigades of Bulow's corps, that have been joined there by BLUCHER. The latter has just risen from the bed to which he has been confined since the battle of Ligny, two days back. He still looks pale and shaken by the severe fall and trampling he endured near the end of the action.

On the summit the troops halt, and a discussion between BLUCHER and his staff ensues.

The cannonade in the direction of Waterloo is growing more and more violent. BLUCHER, after looking this way and that, decides to fall upon the French right at Plancenoit as soon as he can get there, which will not be yet.

Between this point and that the ground descends steeply to the valley on the spectator's left, where there is a mud-bottomed stream, the Lasne; the slope ascends no less abruptly on the other side towards Plancenoit. It is across this defile alone that the Prussian army can proceed thither- a route of unusual difficulty for artillery; where, moreover, the enemy is suspected of having placed a strong outpost during the night to intercept such an approach.

A figure goes forward—that of MAJOR FALKENHAUSEN, who is sent to reconnoitre, and they wait a tedious time, the firing at Waterloo growing more tremendous. FALKENHAUSEN comes back with the welcome news that no outpost is there.

There now remains only the difficulty of the defile itself; and the attempt is made. BLUCHER is descried riding hither and thither as the guns drag heavily down the slope into the muddy bottom of the valley. Here the wheels get stuck, and the men already tired by marching since five in the morning, seem inclined to leave the guns where they are. But the thunder from Waterloo still goes on, BLUCHER exhorts his men by words and eager gestures, and they do at length get the guns across, though with much loss of time.

The advance-guard now reaches some thick trees called the Wood of Paris. It is followed by the LOSTHIN and HILLER divisions of foot, and in due course by the remainder of the two brigades. Here they halt, and await the arrival of the main body of BULOW'S corps, and the third corps under THIELEMANN.

The scene shifts.

SCENE IV

THE FIELD OF WATERLOO. THE ENGLISH POSITION

[WELLINGTON, on Copenhagen, is again under the elm-tree behind La Haye Sainte. Both horse and rider are covered with mud-splashes, but the weather having grown finer the DUKE has taken off his cloak.

UXBRIDGE, FITZROY SOMERSET, CLINTON, ALTEN, COLVILLE, DE LANCEY, HERVEY, GORDON, and other of his staff officers and aides are near him; there being also present GENERALS MUFFLING, HUGEL, and ALAVA; also TYLER, PICTON'S aide. The roar of battle continues.]

WELLINGTON
I am grieved at losing Picton; more than grieved.
He was as grim a devil as ever lived,
And roughish-mouthed withal. But never a man
More stout in fight, more stoical in blame!

TYLER
Before he left for this campaign he said,
"When you shall hear of MY death, mark my words,
You'll hear of a bloody day!" and, on my soul,
'Tis true.

[Enter another aide-de-camp.]

AIDE
Sir William Ponsonby, my lords, has fallen.
His horse got mud-stuck in a new-plowed plot,
Lancers surrounded him and bore him down,
And six then ran him through. The occasion sprung
Mainly from the Brigade's too reckless rush,
Sheer to the French front line.

WELLINGTON [gravely]
Ah—so it comes!
The Greys were bound to pay—'tis always so—

Full dearly for their dash so far afield.
Valour unballasted but lands its freight
On the enemy's shore.—What has become of Hill?

AIDE
We have not seen him latterly, your Grace.

WELLINGTON
By God, I hope I haven't lost him, too?

BRIDGMAN [just come up]
Lord Hill's bay charger, being shot dead, your Grace,
Rolled over him in falling. He is bruised,
But hopes to be in place again betimes.

WELLINGTON
Praise Fate for thinking better of that frown!

[It is now nearing four o'clock. La Haye Sainte is devastated by the second attack of NEY. The farm has
been enveloped by DONZELOT'S division, its garrison, the King's German Legion, having fought till all
ammunition was exhausted. The gates are forced open, and in the retreat of the late defenders to the
main Allied line they are nearly all cut or shot down.]

SPIRIT OF THE PITIES
O Farm of sad vicissitudes and strange!
Farm of the Holy Hedge, yet fool of change!
Whence lit so sanct a name on thy now violate grange?

WELLINGTON [to Muffling, resolutely]
Despite their fierce advantage here, I swear
By every God that war can call upon
To hold our present place at any cost,
Until your force cooperate with our lines!
To that I stand; although 'tis bruited now
That Bulow's corps has only reached Ohain.
I've sent Freemantle hence to seek them there,
And give them inkling we shall need them soon.

MUFFLING [looking at his watch]
I had hoped that Blucher would be here ere this.

[The staff turn their glasses on the French position.]

UXBRIDGE
What movement can it be they contemplate?

WELLINGTON
A shock of cavalry on the hottest scale,

It seems to me.... [To aide] Bid him to reinforce
The front line with some second-line brigades;
Some, too, from the reserve.

[The Brunswickers advance to support MAITLAND'S Guards, and the MITCHELL and ADAM Brigades
establish themselves above Hougomont, which is still in flames.

NEY, in continuation of the plan of throwing his whole force on the British centre before the advent of
the Prussians, now intensifies his onslaught with the cavalry. Terrific discharges of artillery initiate it to
clear the ground. A heavy round-shot dashes through the tree over the heads of WELLINGTON and his
generals, and boughs and leaves come flying down on them.]

WELLINGTON
Good practice that! I vow they did not fire
So dexterously in Spain. [He calls up an aide.] Bid Ompteda
Direct the infantry to lie tight down
On the reverse ridge-slope, to screen themselves
While these close shots and shells are teasing us;
When the charge comes they'll cease.

[The order is carried out. NEY'S cavalry attack now matures. MILHAUD'S cuirassiers in twenty-four
squadrons advance down the opposite decline, followed and supported by seven squadrons of
chasseurs under DESNOETTES. They disappear for a minute in the hollow between the armies.]

UXBRIDGE
Ah—now we have got their long-brewed plot explained!

WELLINGTON [nodding]
That this was rigged for some picked time to-day
I had inferred. But that it would be risked
Sheer on our lines, while still they stand unswayed,
In conscious battle-trim, I reckoned not.
It looks a madman's cruel enterprise!

FITZROY SOMERSET
We have just heard that Ney embarked on it
Without an order, ere its aptness riped.

WELLINGTON
It may be so: he's rash. And yet I doubt.
I know Napoleon. If the onset fail
It will be Ney's; if it succeed he'll claim it!

[A dull reverberation of the tread of innumerable hoofs comes from behind the hill, and the foremost
troops rise into view.]

SPIRIT OF THE PITIES
Behold the gorgeous coming of those horse,

Accoutered in kaleidoscopic hues
That would persuade us war has beauty in it!—
Discern the troopers' mien; each with the air
Of one who is himself a tragedy:
The cuirassiers, steeled, mirroring the day;
Red lancers, green chasseurs: behind the blue
The red; the red before the green:
A lingering-on till late in Christendom,
Of the barbaric trick to terrorize
The foe by aspect!

[WELLINGTON directs his glass to an officer in a rich uniform with many decorations on his breast, who rides near the front of the approaching squadrons. The DUKE'S face expresses admiration.]

WELLINGTON
It's Marshal Ney himself who heads the charge.
The finest cavalry commander, he,
That wears a foreign plume; ay, probably
The whole world through!

SPIRIT IRONIC
And when that matchless chief
Sentenced shall lie to ignominious death
But technically deserved, no finger he
Who speaks will lift to save him.!

SPIRIT OF THE PITIES
To his shame.
We must discount war's generous impulses
I sadly see.

SPIRIT OF THE YEARS
Be mute, and let spin on
This whirlwind of the Will!

[As NEY'S cavalry ascends the English position the swish of the horses' breasts through the standing corn can be heard, and the reverberation of hoofs increases in strength. The English gunners stand with their portfires ready, which are seen glowing luridly in the daylight. There is comparative silence.]

A VOICE
Now, captains, are you loaded?

CAPTAINS
Yes, my lord.

VOICE
Point carefully, and wait till their whole height
Shows above the ridge.

[When the squadrons rise in full view, within sixty yards of the cannon-mouths, the batteries fire, with a concussion that shakes the hill itself. Their shot punch holes through the front ranks of the cuirassiers, and horse and riders fall in heaps. But they are not stopped, hardly checked, galloping up to the mouths of the guns, passing between the pieces, and plunging among the Allied infantry behind the ridge, who, with the advance of the horsemen, have sprung up from their prone position and formed into squares.]

SPIRIT OF RUMOUR
Ney guides the fore-front of the carabineers
Through charge and charge, with rapid recklessness.
Horses, cuirasses, sabres, helmets, men,
Impinge confusedly on the pointed prongs
Of the English kneeling there, whose dim red shapes
Behind their slanted steel seem trampled flat
And sworded to the sward. The charge recedes,
And lo, the tough lines rank there as before,
Save that they are shrunken.

SPIRIT OF THE PITIES
Hero of heroes, too,
Ney, [not forgetting those who gird against him].—
Simple and single-souled lieutenant he;
Why should men's many-valued motions take
So barbarous a groove!

[The cuirassiers and lancers surge round the English and Allied squares like waves, striking furiously on them and well-nigh breaking them. They stand in dogged silence amid the French cheers.]

WELLINGTON [to the nearest square]
Hard pounding this, my men! I truly trust
You'll pound the longest!

SQUARE
Hip-hip-hip-hurrah!

MUFFLING [again referring to his watch]
However firmly they may stand, in faith,
Their firmness must have bounds to it, because
There are bounds to human strength!... Your, Grace,
To leftward now, to spirit Zieten on.

WELLINGTON
Good. It is time! I think he well be late,
However, in the field.

[MUFFLING goes. Enter an aide, breathless.]

AIDE

Your Grace, the Ninety-fifth are patience-spent
With standing under fire so passing long.
They writhe to charge—or anything but stand!

WELLINGTON
Not yet. They shall have at 'em later on.
At present keep them firm.

[Exit aide. The Allied squares stand like little red-brick castles, independent of each other, and
motionless except at the dry hurried command "Close up!" repeated every now and then as they are
slowly thinned. On the other hand, under their firing and bayonets a disorder becomes apparent among
the charging horse, on whose cuirasses the bullets snap like stones on window-panes. At this the Allied
cavalry waiting in the rear advance; and by degrees they deliver the squares from their enemies, who
are withdrawn to their own position to prepare for a still more strenuous assault. The point of view
shifts.]

SCENE V

THE SAME. THE WOMEN'S CAMP NEAR MONT SAINT-JEAN

[On the sheltered side of a clump of trees at the back of the English position camp-fires are smouldering.
Soldiers' wives, mistresses, and children from a few months to five or six years of age, sit on the ground
round the fires or on armfuls of straw from the adjoining farm. Wounded soldiers lie near the women.

The wind occasionally brings the smoke and smell of battle into the encampment, the noise being
continuous. Two waggons stand near; also a surgeon's horse in charge of a batman, laden with bone-
saws, knives, probes, tweezers, and other surgical instruments. Behind lies a woman who has just given
birth to a child, which a second woman is holding.

Many of the other women are shredding lint, the elder children assisting. Some are dressing the slighter
wounds of the soldiers who have come in here instead of going further. Along the road near is a
continual procession of bearers of wounded men to the rear. The occupants of the camp take hardly
any notice of the thundering of the cannon. A camp-follower is playing a fiddle near. Another woman
enters.]

WOMAN
There's no sign of my husband any longer. His battalion is half-a-mile from where it was. He looked
back as they wheeled off towards the fighting-line, as much as to say, "Nancy, if I don't see 'ee again,
this is good-bye, my dear." Yes, poor man!... Not but what 'a had a temper at times!

SECOND WOMAN
I'm out of all that. My husband—as I used to call him for form's sake—is quiet enough. He was
wownded at Quarter-Brass the day before yesterday, and died the same night. But I didn't know it till I
got here, and then says I, "Widder or no widder, I mean to see this out."

[A sergeant staggers in with blood dropping from his face.]

SERGEANT
Damned if I think you will see it out, mis'ess, for if I don't mistake there'll be a retreat of the whole army on Brussels soon. We can't stand much longer!—For the love of God, have ye got a cup of water, if nothing stronger? [They hand a cup.]

THIRD WOMAN [entering and sinking down]
The Lord send that I may never see again what I've been seeing while looking for my poor galliant Joe! The surgeon asked me to lend a hand; and 'twas worse than opening innerds at a pig-killing!

[She faints.]

FOURTH WOMAN [to a little girl]
Never mind her, my dear; come and help me with this one. [She goes with the girl to a soldier in red with buff facings who lies some distance off.] Ah—'tis no good. He's gone.

GIRL
No, mother. His eyes are wide open, a-staring to get a sight of the battle!

FOURTH WOMAN
That's nothing. Lots of dead ones stare in that silly way. It depends upon where they were hit. I was all through the Peninsula; that's how I know. [She covers the horny gaze of the man. Shouts and louder discharges are heard.]—Heaven's high tower, what's that?

[Enter an officer's servant. (5)]

SERVANT
Waiting with the major's spare hoss—up to my knees in mud from the rain that had come down like baccy-pipe stems all the night and morning—I have just seen a charge never beholded since the days of the Amalekites! The squares still stand, but Ney's cavalry have made another attack. Their swords are streaming with blood, and their horses' hoofs squash out our poor fellow's bowels as they lie. A ball has sunk in Sir Thomas Picton's forehead and killed him like Goliath the Philistine. I don't see what's to stop the French. Well, it's the Lord's doing and marvellous in our eyes. Hullo, who's he? [They look towards the road.] A fine hale old gentleman, isn't he? What business has a man of that sort here?

[Enter, on the highway near, the DUKE OF RICHMOND in plain clothes, on horseback, accompanied by two youths, his sons. They draw rein on an eminence, and gaze towards the battlefields.]

RICHMOND [to son]
Everything looks as bad as possible just now. I wonder where your brother is? However, we can't go any nearer.... Yes, the bat-horses are already being moved off, and there are more and more fugitives. A ghastly finish to your mother's ball, by Gad if it isn't!

[They turn their horses towards Brussels. Enter, meeting them, MR. LEGH, a Wessex gentleman, also come out to view the battle.]

LEGH
Can you tell me, sir, how the battle is going?

RICHMOND
Badly, badly, I fear, sir. There will be a retreat soon, seemingly.

LEGH
Indeed! Yes, a crowd of fugitives are coming over the hill even now.
What will these poor women do?

RICHMOND
God knows! They will be ridden over, I suppose. Though it is extraordinary how they do contrive to
escape destruction while hanging so close to the rear of an action! They are moving, however. Well, we
will move too.

[Exeunt DUKE OF RICHMOND, sons, and MR. LEGH. The point of view shifts.]

SCENE VI

THE SAME. THE FRENCH POSITION

[NEY'S charge of cavalry against the opposite upland has been three times renewed without success. He
collects the scattered squadrons to renew it a fourth time. The glittering host again ascends the
confronting slopes over the bodies of those previously left there, and amid horses wandering about
without riders, or crying as they lie with entrails trailing or limbs broken.]

NAPOLEON [starting up]

A horrible dream has gripped me—horrible!
I saw before me Lannes—just as he looked
That day at Aspern: mutilated, bleeding!
"What—blood again?" he said to me. "Still blood?"

[He further arouses himself, takes snuff vehemently, and looks through his glass.]

What time is it?—Ah, these assaults of Ney's!
They are a blunder; they've been enterprised
An hour too early!... There Lheritier goes
Onward with his division next Milhaud;
Now Kellermann must follow up with his.
So one mistake makes many. Yes; ay; yes!

SOULT
I fear that Ney has compromised us here
Just as at Jena; even worse!

NAPOLEON
No less
Must we support him now he is launched on it....

The miracle is that he is still alive!

[NEY and his mass of cavalry again pass the English batteries and disappear amid the squares beyond.]

Their cannon are abandoned; and their squares
Again environed—see! I would to God
Murat could be here! Yet I disdained
His proffered service.... All my star asks now
Is to break some half-dozen of those blocks
Of English yonder. He was the man to do it.

[NEY and D'ERLON'S squadrons are seen emerging from the English squares in a disorganized state, the attack having failed like the previous ones. An aide-de-camp enters to NAPOLEON.]

AIDE
The Prussians have debouched on our right rear
From Paris-wood; and Losthin's infantry
Appear by Plancenoit; Hiller's to leftwards.
Two regiments of their horse protect their front,
And three light batteries.

[A haggard shade crosses NAPOLEON'S face.]

NAPOLEON
What then! That's not a startling force as yet.
A counter-stroke by Domon's cavalry
Must shatter them. Lobau must bring his foot
Up forward, heading for the Prussian front,
Unrecking losses by their cannonade.

[Exit aide. The din of battle continues. DOMON'S horse are soon seen advancing towards and attacking the Prussian hussars in front of the infantry; and he next attempts to silence the Prussian batteries playing on him by leading up his troops and cutting down the gunners. But he has to fall back upon the infantry of LOBAU. Enter another aide-de-camp.]

AIDE
These tiding I report, your Majesty:—
Von Ryssel's and von Hacke's Prussian foot
Have lately sallied from the Wood of Paris,
Bearing on us; no vast array as yet;
But twenty thousand loom not far behind
These vanward marchers!

NAPOLEON
Ah! They swarm thus thickly?
But be they hell's own legions we'll defy them!—
Lobau's men will stand firm.

[He looks in the direction of the English lines, where NEY'S cavalry-assaults still linger furiously on.]

But who rides hither,
Spotting the sky with clods in his high haste?

SOULT
It looks like Colonel Heymes—come from Ney.

NAPOLEON [sullenly]
And his face shows what clef his music's in!

[Enter COLONEL HEYMES, blood-stained, muddy, and breathless.]

HEYMES
The Prince of Moscow, sire, the Marshal Ney,
Bids me implore that infantry be sent
Immediately, to further his attack.
They cannot be dispensed with, save we fail!

NAPOLEON [furiously]
Infantry! Where the sacred God thinks he
I can find infantry for him! Forsooth,
Does he expect me to create them—eh?
Why sends he such a message, seeing well
How we are straitened here!

HEYMES
Such was the prayer
Of my commission, sire. And I say
That I myself have seen his strokes must waste
Without such backing.

NAPOLEON
Why?

HEYMES
Our cavalry
Lie stretched in swathes, fronting the furnace-throats
Of the English cannon as a breastwork built
Of reeking copses. Marshal Ney's third horse
Is shot. Besides the slain, Donop, Guyot,
Lheritier, Piquet, Travers, Delort, more,
Are vilely wounded. On the other hand
Wellington has sought refuge in a square,
Few of his generals are not killed or hit,
And all is tickle with him. But I see,
Likewise, that I can claim no reinforcement,
And will return and say so.

[Exit HEYMES]

NAPOLEON [to Soult, sadly]
Ney does win me!
I fain would strengthen him.—Within an ace
Of breaking down the English as he is,
'Twould write upon the sunset "Victory!"—
But whom may spare we from the right here now?
So single man!

[An interval.]

Life's curse begins, I see,
With helplessness!... All I can compass is
To send Durutte to fall on Papelotte,
And yet more strongly occupy La Haye,
To cut off Bulow's right from bearing up
And checking Ney's attack. Further than this
None but the Gods can scheme!

[SOULT hastily begins writing orders to that effect. The point of view shifts.]

SCENE VII

THE SAME. THE ENGLISH POSITION

[The din of battle continues. WELLINGTON, UXBRIDGE, HILL, DE LANCEY, GORDON, and others
discovered near the middle of the line.]

SPIRIT OF RUMOUR
It is a moment when the steadiest pulse
Thuds pit-a-pat. The crisis shapes and nears
For Wellington as for his counter-chief.

SPIRIT OF THE PITIES
The hour is shaking him, unshakeable
As he may seem!

SPIRIT OF THE YEARS
Know'st not at this stale time
That shaken and unshaken are alike
But demonstrations from the Back of Things?
Must I again reveal It as It hauls
The halyards of the world?

[A transparency as in earlier scenes again pervades the spectacle, and the ubiquitous urging of the Immanent Will becomes visualized. The web connecting all the apparently separate shapes includes WELLINGTON in its tissue with the rest, and shows him, like them, as acting while discovering his intention to act. By the lurid light the faces of every row, square, group, and column of men, French and English, wear the expression of that of people in a dream.]

SPIRIT OF THE PITIES [tremulously]
Yea, sire; I see.
Disquiet me, pray, no more!

[The strange light passes, and the embattled hosts on the field seem to move independently as usual.]

WELLINGTON [to Uxbridge]
Manoeuvring does not seem to animate
Napoleon's methods now. Forward he comes,
And pounds away on us in the ancient style,
Till he is beaten back in the ancient style;
And so the see-saw sways!

[The din increases. WELLINGTON'S aide-de-camp, Sir A. GORDON, a little in his rear, falls mortally wounded. The DUKE turns quickly.]

But where is Gordon?
Ah—hit is he! That's bad, that's bad, by God.

[GORDON is removed. An aide enters.]

AIDE
Your Grace, the Colonel Ompteda has fallen,
And La Haye Sainte is now a bath of blood.
Nothing more can be done there, save with help.
The Rifles suffer sharply!

[An aide is seen coming from KEMPT.]

WELLINGTON
What says he?

DE LANCEY
He says that Kempt, being riddled through and thinned,
Sends him for reinforcements.

WELLINGTON [with heat]
Reinforcements?
And where am I to get him reinforcements
In Heaven's name! I've no reinforcements here,
As he should know.

AIDE [hesitating]
What's to be done, your Grace?

WELLINGTON
Done? Those he has left him, be they many or few,
Fight till they fall, like others in the field!

[Exit aide. The Quartermaster-General DE LANCEY, riding by WELLINGTON, is struck by a lobbing shot that hurls him over the head of his horse. WELLINGTON and others go to him.]

DE LANCEY [faintly]
I may as well be left to die in peace!

WELLINGTON
He may recover. Take him to the rear,
And call the best attention up to him.

[DE LANCEY is carried off. The next moment a shell bursts close to WELLINGTON.]

HILL [approaching]
I strongly feel you stand too much exposed!
WELLINGTON

I know, I know. It matters not one damn!
I may as well be shot as not perceive
What ills are raging here.

HILL
Conceding such,
And as you may be ended momently,
A truth there is no blinking, what commands
Have you to leave me, should fate shape it so?

WELLINGTON
These simply: to hold out unto the last,
As long as one man stands on one lame leg
With one ball in his pouch!—then end as I.

[He rides on slowly with the others. NEY'S charges, though fruitless so far, are still fierce. His troops are now reduced to one-half. Regiments of the BACHELU division, and the JAMIN brigade, are at last moved up to his assistance. They are partly swept down by the Allied batteries, and partly notched away by the infantry, the smoke being now so thick that the position of the battalions is revealed only by the flashing of the priming-pans and muzzles, and by the furious oaths heard behind the cloud.

WELLINGTON comes back. Enter another aide-de-camp.]

AIDE
We bow to the necessity of saying

That our brigade is lessened to one-third,
Your Grace. And those who are left alive of it
Are so unmuscled by fatigue and thirst
That some relief, however temporary,
Becomes sore need.

WELLINGTON
Inform your general
That his proposal asks the impossible!
That he, I, every Englishman afield,
Must fall upon the spot we occupy,
Our wounds in front.

AIDE
It is enough, your Grace.
I answer for't that he, those under him,
And I withal, will bear us as you say.

[Exit aide. The din of battle goes on. WELLINGTON is grave but calm. Like those around him, he is splashed to the top of his hat with partly dried mire, mingled with red spots; his face is grimed in the same way, little courses showing themselves where the sweat has trickled down from his brow and temples.]

CLINTON [to Hill]
A rest would do our chieftain no less good,
In faith, than that unfortunate brigade!
He is tried damnably; and much more strained
Than I have ever seen him.

HILL
Endless risks
He's running likewise. What the hell would happen
If he were shot, is more than I can say!

WELLINGTON [calling to some near]
At Talavera, Salamanca, boys,
And at Vitoria, we saw smoke together;
And though the day seems wearing doubtfully,
Beaten we must not be! What would they say
Of us at home, if so?
A CRY [from the French]

Their centre breaks!
Vive l'Empereur!

[It comes from the FOY and BACHELU divisions, which are rushing forward. HALKETT'S and DUPLAT'S brigades intercept. DUPLAT falls, shot dead; but the venturesome French regiments, pierced with converging fires, and cleft with shells, have to retreat.]

HILL [joining Wellington]
The French artillery-fire
To the right still renders regiments restive there
That have to stand. The long exposure galls them.

WELLINGTON
They must be stayed as our poor means afford.
I have to bend attention steadfastly
Upon the centre here. The game just now
Goes all against us; and if staunchness fail
But for one moment with these thinning foot,
Defeat succeeds!

[The battle continues to sway hither and thither with concussions, wounds, smoke, the fumes of gunpowder, and the steam from the hot viscera of grape-torn horses and men. One side of a Hanoverian square is blown away; the three remaining sides form themselves into a triangle. So many of his aides are cut down that it is difficult for WELLINGTON to get reports of what is happening afar. It begins to be discovered at the front that a regiment of hussars, and others without ammunition, have deserted, and that some officers in the rear, honestly concluding the battle to be lost, are riding quietly off to Brussels. Those who are left unwounded of WELLINGTON'S staff show gloomy misgivings at such signs, despite their own firmness.]

SPIRIT SINISTER
One needs must be a ghost
To move here in the midst 'twixt host and host!
Their balls scream brisk and breezy tunes through me
As I were an organ-stop. It's merry so;
What damage mortal flesh must undergo!

[A Prussian officer enters to MUFFLING, who has again rejoined the DUKE'S suite. MUFFLING hastens forward to WELLINGTON.]

MUFFLING
Blucher has just begun to operate;
But owing to Gneisenau's stolid stagnancy
The body of our army looms not yet!
As Zieten's corps still plod behind Smohain
Their coming must be late. Blucher's attack
Strikes the remote right rear of the enemy,
Somewhere by Plancenoit.

WELLINGTON
A timely blow;
But would that Zieten sped! Well, better late
Than never. We'll still stand.

[The point of observation shifts.]

SCENE VIII

THE SAME. LATER

[NEY'S long attacks on the centre with cavalry having failed, those left of the squadrons and their infantry-supports fall back pell-mell in broken groups across the depression between the armies.

Meanwhile BULOW, having engaged LOBAU'S Sixth Corps, carries Plancenoit.

The artillery-fire between the French and the English continues. An officer of the Third Foot-guards comes up to WELLINGTON and those of his suite that survive.]

OFFICER
Our Colonel Canning—coming I know not whence—

WELLINGTON
I lately sent him with important words
To the remoter lines.

OFFICER
As he returned
A grape-shot struck him in the breast; he fell,
At once a dead man. General Halkett, too,
Has had his cheek shot through, but still keeps going.

WELLINGTON
And how proceeds De Lancey?

OFFICER
I am told
That he forbids the surgeons waste their time
On him, who well can wait till worse are eased.

WELLINGTON
A noble fellow.

[NAPOLEON can now be seen, across the valley, pushing forward a new scheme of some sort, urged to it obviously by the visible nearing of further Prussian corps. The EMPEROR is as critically situated as WELLINGTON, and his army is now formed in a right angle ["en potence"], the main front to the English, the lesser to as many of the Prussians as have yet arrived. His gestures show him to be giving instructions of desperate import to a general whom he has called up.]

SPIRIT IRONIC
He bids La Bedoyere to speed away
Along the whole sweep of the surging line,

And there announce to the breath-shotten bands
Who toil for a chimaera trustfully,
With seventy pounds of luggage on their loins,
That the dim Prussian masses seen afar
Are Grouchy's three-and-thirty thousand, come
To clinch a victory.

SPIRIT OF THE PITIES
But Ney demurs!

SPIRIT IRONIC
Ney holds indignantly that such a feint
Is not war-worthy. Says Napoleon then,
Snuffing anew, with sour sardonic scowl,
That he is choiceless.

SPIRIT SINISTER
Excellent Emperor!
He tops all human greatness; in that he
To lesser grounds of greatness adds the prime,
Of being without a conscience.

[LA BEDOYERE and orderlies start on their mission. The false intelligence is seen to spread, by the
excited motion of the columns, and the soldiers can be heard shouting as their spirits revive.

WELLINGTON is beginning to discern the features of the coming onset, when COLONEL FRASER rides
up.]

FRASER
We have just learnt from a deserting captain,
One of the carabineers who charged of late,
That an assault which dwarfs all instances—
The whole Imperial Guard in welded weight—
Is shortly to be made.

WELLINGTON
For your smart speed
My thanks. My observation is confirmed.
We'll hasten now along the battle-line [to Staff],
As swiftest means for giving orders out
Whereby to combat this.

[The speaker, accompanied by HILL, UXBRIDGE, and others—all now looking as worn and besmirched as
the men in the ranks—proceed along the lines, and dispose the brigades to meet the threatened shock.
The infantry are brought out of the shelter they have recently sought, the cavalry stationed in the rear,
and the batteries of artillery hitherto kept in reserve are moved to the front.

The last Act of the battle begins.

There is a preliminary attack by DONZELOT'S columns, combined with swarms of sharpshooters, to the disadvantage of the English and their Allies. WELLINGTON has scanned it closely. FITZROY SOMERSET, his military secretary, comes up.]

WELLINGTON
What casualty has thrown its shade among
The regiments of Nassau, to shake them so?

SOMERSET
The Prince of Orange has been badly struck—
A bullet through his shoulder—so they tell;
And Kielmansegge has shown some signs of stress.
Kincaird's tried line wanes leaner and more lean—
Whittled to a weak skein of skirmishers;
The Twenty-seventh lie dead.

WELLINGTON
Ah yes—I know!

[While they watch developments a cannon-shot passes and knocks SOMERSET'S right arm to a mash. He is assisted to the rear.

NEY and FRIANT now lead forward the last and most desperate assault of the day, in charges of the Old and Middle Guard, the attack by DONZELOT and ALLIX further east still continuing as a support. It is about a quarter-past eight, and the midsummer evening is fine after the wet night and morning, the sun approaching its setting in a sky of gorgeous colours.

The picked and toughened Guard, many of whom stood in the ranks at Austerlitz and Wagram, have been drawn up in three or four echelons, the foremost of which now advances up the slopes to the Allies' position. The others follow at intervals, the drummers beating the "pas de charge."]

CHORUS OF RUMOURS [aerial music]
Twice thirty throats of couchant cannonry—
Ranked in a hollow curve, to close their blaze
Upon the advancing files—wait silently
Like to black bulls at gaze.

The Guard approaches nearer and more near:
To touch-hole moves each match of smoky sheen:
The ordnance roars: the van-ranks disappear
As if wiped off the scene.

The aged Friant falls as it resounds;
Ney's charger drops—his fifth on this sore day—
Its rider from the quivering body bounds
And forward foots his way.

The cloven columns tread the English height,
Seize guns, repulse battalions rank by rank,
While horse and foot artillery heavily bite
Into their front and flank.

It nulls the power of a flesh-built frame
To live within that zone of missiles. Back
The Old Guard, staggering, climbs to whence it came.
The fallen define its track.

[The second echelon of the Imperial Guard has come up to the assault. Its columns have borne upon
HALKETT'S right. HALKETT, desperate to keep his wavering men firm, himself seizes and waves the flag
of the Thirty-third, in which act he falls wounded. But the men rally. Meanwhile the Fifty-second,
covered by the Seventy-first, has advanced across the front, and charges the Imperial Guard on the
flank.

The third echelon next arrives at the English lines and squares; rushes through the very focus of their
fire, and seeing nothing more in front, raises a shout.

IMPERIAL GUARD
The Emperor! It's victory!

WELLINGTON
Stand up, Guards!
Form line upon the front face of the square!

[Two thousand of MAITLAND'S Guards, hidden in the hollow roadway, thereupon spring up, form as
ordered, and reveal themselves as a fence of leveled firelocks four deep. The flints click in a multitude,
the pans flash, and volley after volley is poured into the bear-skinned figures of the massed French, who
kill COLONEL D'OYLEY in returning fire.]

WELLINGTON
Now drive the fellows in! Go on; go on!
You'll do it now!

[COLBORNE converges on the French guard with the Fifty-second, and The former splits into two as the
climax comes. ADAM, MAITLAND, and COLBORNE pursue their advantage. The Imperial columns are
broken, and their confusion is increased by grape-shot from BOLTON'S battery.]

Campbell, this order next:
Vivian's hussars are to support, and bear
Against the cavalry towards Belle Alliance.
Go—let him know.

[Sir C. CAMPBELL departs with the order. Soon VIVIAN'S and VANDELEUR'S light horse are seen
advancing, and in due time the French cavalry are rolled back.

WELLINGTON goes in the direction of the hussars with UXBRIDGE. A cannon-shot hisses past.]

UXBRIDGE [starting]
I have lost my leg, by God!

WELLINGTON
By God, and have you! Ay—the wind o' the shot
Blew past the withers of my Copenhagen
Like the foul sweeping of a witch's broom.—
Aha—they are giving way!

[While UXBRIDGE is being helped to the rear, WELLINGTON makes a sign to SALTOUN, Colonel of the
First Footguards.]

SALTOUN [shouting]
Boys, now's your time;
Forward and win!

FRENCH VOICES
The Guard gives way—we are beaten!

[They recede down the hill, carrying confusion into NAPOLEON'S centre just as the Prussians press
forward at a right angle from the other side of the field. NAPOLEON is seen standing in the hollow
beyond La Haye Sainte, alone, except for the presence of COUNT FLAHAULT, his aide-de-camp. His lips
move with sudden exclamation.

SPIRIT OF THE YEARS
He says "Now all is lost! The clocks of the world
Strike my last empery-hour."

[Towards La Haye Sainte the French of DONZELOT and ALLIX, who are fighting KEMPT, PACK, KRUSE, and
LAMBERT, seeing what has happened to the Old and Middle Guard, lose heart and recede likewise; so
that the whole French line rolls back like a tide. Simultaneously the Prussians are pressing forward at
Papelotte and La Haye. The retreat of the French grows into a panic.]

FRENCH VOICES [despairingly]
We are betrayed!

[WELLINGTON rides at a gallop to the most salient point of the English position, halts, and waves his hat
as a signal to all the army. The sign is answered by a cheer along the length of the line.]

WELLINGTON
No cheering yet, my lads; but bear ahead,
Before the inflamed face of the west out there
Dons blackness. So you'll round your victory!

[The few aides that are left unhurt dart hither and thither with this message, and the whole English host
and it allies advance in an ordered mass down the hill except some of the artillery, who cannot get their
wheels over the bank of corpses in front. Trumpets, drums, and bugles resound with the advance.

The streams of French fugitives as they run are cut down and shot by their pursuers, whose clothes and contracted features are blackened by smoke and cartridge-biting, and soiled with loam and blood. Some French blow out their own brains as they fly. The sun drops below the horizon while the slaughter goes on.]

SPIRIT OF THE PITIES
Is this the last Esdraelon of a moil
For mortal man's effacement?

SPIRIT IRONIC
Warfare, mere,
Plied by the Managed for the Managers;
To wit: by frenzied folks who profit nought
For those who profit all!

SPIRIT OF THE PITIES
Between the jars
Of these who live, I hear uplift and move
The bones of those who placidly have lain
Within the sacred garths of yon grey fanes—
Nivelles, and Plancenoit, and Braine l'Alleud—
Beneath the unmemoried mounds through deedless years
Their dry jaws quake: "What Sabaoath is this,
That shakes us in our unobtrusive shrouds,
As though our tissues did not yet abhor
The fevered feats of life?"

SPIRIT IRONIC
Mere fancy's feints!
How know the coffined what comes after them,
Even though it whirl them to the Pleiades?—
Turn to the real.

SPIRIT OF RUMOUR
That hatless, smoke-smirched shape
There in the vale, is still the living Ney,
His sabre broken in his hand, his clothes
Slitten with ploughing ball and bayonet,
One epaulette shorn away. He calls out "Follow!"
And a devoted handful follow him
Once more into the carnage. Hear his voice.

NEY [calling afar]
My friends, see how a Marshal of France can die!

SPIRIT OF THE PITIES
Alas, not here in battle, something hints,

But elsewhere!... Who's the sworded brother-chief
Swept past him in the tumult?

SPIRIT OF RUMOUR
D'Erlon he.
Ney cries to him:

NEY
Be sure of this, my friend,
If we don't perish here at English hands,
Nothing is left us but the halter-noose
The Bourbons will provide!

SPIRIT IRONIC
A caustic wit,
And apt, to those who deal in adumbrations!

[The brave remnant of the Imperial Guard repulses for a time the English cavalry under Vivian, in which
MAJOR HOWARD and LIEUTENANT GUNNING of the Tenth Hussars are shot. But the war-weary French
cannot cope with the pursuing infantry, helped by grape-shot from the batteries.

NAPOLEON endeavours to rally them. It is his last effort as a warrior; and the rally ends feebly.]

NAPOLEON
They are crushed! So it has ever been since Crecy!

[He is thrown violently off his horse, and bids his page bring another, which he mounts, and is lost to
sight.]

SPIRIT OF RUMOUR
He loses his last chance of dying well!

[The three or four heroic battalions of the Old and Middle Guard fall back step by step, halting to reform
in square when they get badly broken and shrunk. At last they are surrounded by the English Guards
and other foot, who keep firing on them and smiting them to smaller and smaller numbers. GENERAL
CAMBRONNE is inside the square.]

COLONEL HUGH HALKETT [shouting]
Surrender! And preserve those heroes' lives!

CAMBRONNE [with exasperation]
Mer-r-rde!... You've to deal with desperates, man, today:
Life is a byword here!

[Hollow laughter, as from people in hell, comes approvingly from the remains of the Old Guard. The
English proceed with their massacre, the devoted band thins and thins, and a ball strikes CAMBRONNE,
who falls, and is trampled over.]

SPIRIT OF THE YEARS
Observe that all wide sight and self-command
Desert these throngs now driven to demonry
By the Immanent Unrecking. Nought remains
But vindictiveness here amid the strong,
And there amid the weak an impotent rage.

SPIRIT OF THE PITIES
Why prompts the Will so senseless-shaped a doing?

SPIRIT OF THE YEARS
I have told thee that It works unwittingly,
As one possessed, not judging.

SEMICHORUS I OF IRONIC SPIRITS [aerial music]
Of Its doings if It knew,
What It does It would not do!

SEMICHORUS II
Since It knows not, what far sense
Speeds Its spinnings in the Immense?

SEMICHORUS I
None; a fixed foresightless dream
Is Its whole philosopheme.

SEMICHORUS II
Just so; an unconscious planning,
Like a potter raptly panning!

CHORUS
Are then, Love and Light Its aim—
Good Its glory, Bad Its blame?
Nay; to alter evermore
Things from what they were before.

SPIRIT OF THE YEARS
Your knowings of the Unknowable declared,
Let the last pictures of the play be bared.

[Enter, fighting, more English and Prussians against the French. NEY is caught by the throng and borne ahead. RULLIERE hides an eagle beneath his coat and follows Ney. NAPOLEON is involved none knows where in the crowd of fugitives.

WELLINGTON and BLUCHER come severally to the view. They meet in the dusk and salute warmly. The Prussian bands strike up "God save the King" as the two shake hands. From his gestures of assent it can be seen that WELLINGTON accepts BLUCHER'S offer to pursue.

The reds disappear from the sky, and the dusk grows deeper. The action of the battle degenerates to a hunt, and recedes further and further into the distance southward. When the tramplings and shouts of the combatants have dwindled, the lower sounds are noticeable that come from the wounded: hopeless appeals, cries for water, elaborate blasphemies, and impotent execrations of Heaven and hell. In the vast and dusky shambles black slouching shapes begin to move, the plunderers of the dead and dying.

The night grows clear and beautiful, and the moon shines musingly down. But instead of the sweet smell of green herbs and dewy rye as at her last beaming upon these fields, there is now the stench of gunpowder and a muddy stew of crushed crops and gore.]

SPIRIT OF THE YEARS
So hath the Urging Immanence used to-day
Its inadvertent might to field this fray:
And Europe's wormy dynasties rerobe
Themselves in their old gilt, to dazzle anew the globe!

[The scene us curtained by a night-mist. (6)]

SCENE IX

THE WOOD OF BOSSU

[It is midnight. NAPOLEON enters a glade of the wood, a solitary figure on a faded horse. The shadows of the boughs travel over his listless form as he moves along. The horse chooses its own path, comes to a standstill, and feeds. The tramp of BERTRAND, SOULT, DROUOT, and LOBAU'S horses, gone forward in hope to find a way of retreat, is heard receding over the hill.]

NAPOLEON [to himself, languidly]
Here should have been some troops of Gerard's corps,
Left to protect the passage of the convoys,
Yet they, too, fail.... I have nothing more to lose,
But life!

[Flocks of fugitive soldiers pass along the adjoining road without seeing him. NAPOLEON'S head droops lower and lower as he sits listless in the saddle, and he falls into a fitful sleep. The moon shines upon his face, which is drawn and waxen.]

SPIRIT OF THE YEARS
"Sic diis immortalibus placet,"—
"Thus is it pleasing to the immortal gods,"
As earthlings used to say. Thus, to this last,
The Will in thee has moved thee, Bonaparte,
As we say now.

NAPOLEON [starting]
Whose frigid tones are those,

Breaking upon my lurid loneliness
So brusquely?... Yet, 'tis true, I have ever know
That such a Will I passively obeyed!

[He drowses again.]

SPIRIT IRONIC
Nothing care I for these high-doctrined dreams,
And shape the case in quite a common way,
So I would ask, Ajaccian Bonaparte,
Has all this been worth while?

NAPOLEON
O hideous hour,
Why am I stung by spectral questionings?
Did not my clouded soul incline to match
Those of the corpses yonder, thou should'st rue
Thy saying, Fiend, whoever those may'st be!...

Why did the death-drops fail to bite me close
I took at Fontainebleau? Had I then ceased,
This deep had been umplumbed; had they but worked,
I had thrown threefold the glow of Hannibal
Down History's dusky lanes!—Is it too late?...
Yes. Self-sought death would smoke but damply here!

If but a Kremlin cannon-shot had met me
My greatness would have stood: I should have scored
A vast repute, scarce paralleled in time.
As it did not, the fates had served me best
If in the thick and thunder of to-day,
Like Nelson, Harold, Hector, Cyrus, Saul,
I had been shifted from this jail of flesh,
To wander as a greatened ghost elsewhere.
—Yes, a good death, to have died on yonder field;
But never a ball came padding down my way!

So, as it is, a miss-mark they will dub me;
And yet—I found the crown of France in the mire,
And with the point of my prevailing sword
I picked it up! But for all this and this
I shall be nothing....
To shoulder Christ from out the topmost niche
In human fame, as once I fondly felt,
Was not for me. I came too late in time
To assume the prophet or the demi-god,
A part past playing now. My only course
To make good showance to posterity

Was to implant my line upon the throne.
And how shape that, if now extinction nears?
Great men are meteors that consume themselves
To light the earth. This is my burnt-out hour.

SPIRIT OF THE YEARS
Thou sayest well. Thy full meridian-shine
Was in the glory of the Dresden days,
When well-nigh every monarch throned in Europe
Bent at thy footstool.

NAPOLEON
Saving always England's—
Rightly dost say "well-nigh."—Not England's,—she
Whose tough, enisled, self-centred, kindless craft
Has tracked me, springed me, thumbed me by the throat,
And made herself the means of mangling me!

SPIRIT IRONIC
Yea, the dull peoples and the Dynasts both,
Those counter-castes not oft adjustable,
Interests antagonistic, proud and poor,
Have for the nonce been bonded by a wish
To overthrow thee.

SPIRIT OF THE PITIES
Peace. His loaded heart
Bears weight enough for one bruised, blistered while!

SPIRIT OF THE YEARS
Worthless these kneadings of thy narrow thought,
Napoleon; gone thy opportunity!
Such men as thou, who wade across the world
To make an epoch, bless, confuse, appal,
Are in the elemental ages' chart
Like meanest insects on obscurest leaves,
But incidents and grooves of Earth's unfolding;
Or as the brazen rod that stirs the fire
Because it must.

[The moon sinks, and darkness blots out NAPOLEON and the scene.]

AFTER SCENE

THE OVERWORLD

[Enter the Spirit and Chorus of the Years, the Spirit and Chorus of the Pities, the Shade of the Earth, the Spirits Sinister and Ironic with their Choruses, Rumours, Spirit-messengers and Recording Angels.

Europe has now sunk netherward to its far-off position as in the Fore Scene, and it is beheld again as a prone and emaciated figure of which the Alps form the vertebrae, and the branching mountain-chains the ribs, the Spanish Peninsula shaping the head of the ecorche. The lowlands look like a grey-green garment half-thrown off, and the sea around like a disturbed bed on which the figure lies.]

SPIRIT OF THE YEARS
Thus doth the Great Foresightless mechanize
In blank entrancement now as evermore
Its ceaseless artistries in Circumstance
Of curious stuff and braid, as just forthshown.

Yet but one flimsy riband of Its web
Have we here watched in weaving—web Enorm,
Whose furthest hem and selvage may extend
To where the roars and plashings of the flames
Of earth-invisible suns swell noisily,
And onwards into ghastly gulfs of sky,
Where hideous presences churn through the dark—
Monsters of magnitude without a shape,
Hanging amid deep wells of nothingness.

Yet seems this vast and singular confection
Wherein our scenery glints of scantest size,
Inutile all—so far as reasonings tell.

SPIRIT OF THE PITIES
Thou arguest still the Inadvertent Mind.—
But, even so, shall blankness be for aye?
Men gained cognition with the flux of time,
And wherefore not the Force informing them,
When far-ranged aions past all fathoming
Shall have swung by, and stand as backward years?

SPIRIT OF THE YEARS
What wouldst have hoped and had the Will to be?—
How wouldst have paeaned It, if what hadst dreamed
Thereof were truth, and all my showings dream?

SPIRIT OF THE PITIES
The Will that fed my hope was far from thine,
One I would thus have hymned eternally:—

SEMICHORUS I OF THE PITIES [aerial music]
To Thee whose eye all Nature owns,
Who hurlest Dynasts from their thrones, (7)

And liftest those of low estate
We sing, with Her men consecrate!

SEMICHORUS II
Yea, Great and Good, Thee, Thee we hail,
Who shak'st the strong, Who shield'st the frail,
Who hadst not shaped such souls as we
If tendermercy lacked in Thee!

SEMICHORUS I
Though times be when the mortal moan
Seems unascending to Thy throne,
Though seers do not as yet explain
Why Suffering sobs to Thee in vain;

SEMICHORUS II
We hold that Thy unscanted scope
Affords a food for final Hope,
That mild-eyed Prescience ponders nigh
Life's loom, to lull it by-and-by.

SEMICHORUS I
Therefore we quire to highest height
The Wellwiller, the kindly Might
That balances the Vast for weal,
That purges as by wounds to heal.

SEMICHORUS II
The systemed suns the skies enscroll
Obey Thee in their rhythmic roll,
Ride radiantly at Thy command,
Are darkened by Thy Masterhand!

SEMICHORUS I
And these pale panting multitudes
Seen surging here, their moils, their moods,
All shall "fulfil their joy" in Thee
In Thee abide eternally!

SEMICHORUS II
Exultant adoration give
The Alone, through Whom all living live,
The Alone, in Whom all dying die,
Whose means the End shall justify! Amen.

SPIRIT OF THE PITIES
So did we evermore, sublimely sing;
So would we now, despise thy forthshowing!

SPIRIT OF THE YEARS
Something of difference animates your quiring,
O half-convinced Compassionates and fond,
From chords consistent with our spectacle!
You almost charm my long philosophy
Out of my strong-built thought, and bear me back
To when I thanksgave thus.... Ay, start not, Shades;
In the Foregone I knew what dreaming was,
And could let raptures rule! But not so now.
Yea, I psalmed thus and thus.... But not so now.

SEMICHORUS I OF THE YEARS [aerial music]
O Immanence, That reasonest not
In putting forth all things begot,
Thou build'st Thy house in space—for what?

SEMICHORUS II
O loveless, Hateless!—past the sense
Of kindly eyed benevolence,
To what tune danceth this Immense?

SPIRIT IRONIC
For one I cannot answer. But I know
'Tis handsome of our Pities so to sing
The praises of the dreaming, dark, dumb Thing
That turns the handle of this idle show!

As once a Greek asked I would fain ask too,
Who knows if all the Spectacle be true,
Or an illusion of the gods [the Will,
To wit] some hocus-pocus to fulfil?

SEMICHORUS I OF THE YEARS [aerial music]
Last as first the question rings
Of the Will's long travailings;
Why the All-mover,
Why the All-prover
Ever urges on and measure out the chordless chime of Things. (8)

SEMICHORUS II
Heaving dumbly
As we deem,
Moulding numbly
As in dream
Apprehending not how fare the sentient subjects of Its scheme.

SEMICHORUS I OF THE PITIES

Nay;—shall not Its blindness break?
Yea, must not Its heart awake,
Promptly tending
To Its mending
In a genial germing purpose, and for loving-kindness sake?

SEMICHORUS II
Should it never
Curb or care
Aught whatever
Those endure
Whom It quickens, let them darkle to extinction swift and sure.

CHORUS
But—a stirring thrills the air
Like to sounds of joyance there
That the rages
Of the ages
Shall be cancelled, and deliverance offered from the darts that were,
Consciousness the Will informing, till It fashion all things fair!

THE END OF "THE DYNASTS"

September 25, 1907

FOOTNOTES

(1) - Hussars, it may be remembered, used to wear a pelisse, dolman, or "sling-jacket" [Footnote as the men called: which hung loosely over the shoulder. The writer is able to recall the picturesque effect of this uniform.

(2) - Sheridan.

(3) - This famous ball has become so embedded in the history of the Hundred Days as to be an integral part of it. Yet in spite of the efforts that have been made to locate the room which saw the memorable gathering [Footnote by the present writer more than thirty years back, among other enthusiasts: a dispassionate judgment must deny that its site has as yet been proven. Even Sir W. Fraser is not convincing. The event happened less than a century ago, but the spot is almost as phantasmal in its elusive mystery as towered Camelot, the palace of Priam, or the hill of Calvary.

(4) - The spelling of the date is used.

(5) - Samuel Clark; born 1779, died 1857. Buried at West Stafford, Dorset.

(6 (One of the many Waterloo men known to the writer in his youth, John Bentley of the Fusileer Guards, use to declare that he lay down on the ground in such weariness that when food was brought him he could not eat it, and slept till next morning on an empty stomach. He died at Chelsea Hospital, 187-, aged eighty six.

(7) - This footnote is an excerpt in Greek from the "Magnificat" canticle, the Latin character equivalent being "katheile DYNASTAS apo THrono," or "He has put down the mighty from their thrones."—D.L.

(8) - Hor. Epis. i, 12.

THOMAS HARDY – A SHORT BIOGRAPHY

Thomas Hardy OM was an English novelist, whose Victorian realism was inspired by the Romantic movement, particularly Wordsworth, and by Dickens, who was also critical of much of Victorian society. Unlike Dickens, though, who writes primarily about cities and towns, Hardy sets much of his work in the semi-fictional country of Wessex, focusing on the decline of rural practice in England. He was known first for his novels, but towards the end of his life his poetry began to see publication and he is now considered one of the major poets of English literature, influencing various poets in the 1950-60s, most notably Philip Larkin.

Hardy was born in the hamlet of Upper Bockhampton in the Stinsford parish about three miles east of Dorchester in Dorset, England, on 2nd June 1840, in a two-storey brick and thatch cottage. His father Thomas worked as a self-employed master mason and local builder contractor, while also playing the violin. His mother, Jemima, a former maid-servant and cook, was well-read in Latin and French romances in English translation, and she enjoyed retelling the folk stories and legends of the region while she educated her son until the age of eight when he first attended the local National School in Lower Bockhampton, which had opened that year in 1848. The school was run by the National Society for Promoting the Education of the Poor in the Principles of the Established Church. From his parents, he received all of the interests and passions which would shape his writing and his life; the interest in architecture and love of music from his father, and his interest in rural lifestyles and traditions from his mother, along with a passion for literature. The Hardy family were descended from the Le Hardy family, who had resided on the Isle of Jersey since the 15th century. They had several ancestors of significant import, though at the turn of the eighteenth century the family had experienced a sharp economic collapse, a circumstance which would become key to the narrative of Tess of the d'Urbervilles. Maul Turner writes of Hardy's childhood that "apart from parental influences, Hardy's childhood was dominated by two things: the local church, and the natural world around him".

After two years at the National School, his mother enrolled him at a non-conformist school in Dorchester, run by the British and Foreign School Society, and while there he learnt Latin and French, amongst other subjects. To compliment his education, he read Greek and Roman classics in translation, and the Bible, which he knew in close detail, and he expressed a fondness for romances. In addition to his favourite authors, William Harrison Ainsworth, Walter Scott and Alexandre Dumas, he read

Shakespeare's tragedies and, although ultimately he rather enjoyed school, he preferred to read books in relative solitude. While he was in Dorset, he bore witness to the decline of the traditions of the pastoral society in the face of the rise of industrialism.

Deemed unlikely by his parents and his teachers to lead a successful scholarly or clerical career, Hardy gained an apprenticeship in 1856 at the age of sixteen to John Hicks, a local architect whose speciality was in church restoration. The occupation saw him travelling extensively around Dorset, while back at the office he met another apprentice, Henry Bastow, with a similar interest in classical literature, poetry and religious matters. His only opportunity to read was in the morning before work between the hours of five and eight, and while he was working and reading here he met the poet William Barnes, also a local schoolmaster, who published poetry focusing on rural life in local dialects, and it is quite possible that it was this encounter which encouraged him to write poetry about similar themes. Within this poetry are various ideas which he picked up while on his apprenticeship, and he showed his poetry to Horace Moule, son of the vicar and a student at Queen's College, Cambridge, who, eight years Hardy's senior, became his best friend and mentor and encouraged him in his reading of Greek tragedy and more contemporary English literature. The most significant works of literature published at this time, which will no doubt have influenced Hardy, were Alfred Tennyson's poems Idylls of the King, George Meredith's Richard Feverel and Evan Harrington, Wilkie Collins's The Woman in White and George Eliot's The Mill on the Floss. Alongside these works of fiction was Charles Darwin's The Origin of Species, which had a profound influence on Hardy.

Suspending his architectural apprenticeship and heading for London in April 1862, he rented lodgings at 3, Clarence Place at Kilburn, near the Edgware Road. This move is widely considered to be the result of an unsuccessful love affair; he had already had infatuations with two girls in Dorset, who "scorned him as too young", and just prior to his move he had proposed to and been rejected by a Dorchester girl, Mary Waight, also significantly his senior. These rejections arguably encouraged him to move and begin afresh in new surroundings. While in London, he spent five years working as Arthur Blomfield's assistant architect, a noted restorer and designer of churches. Blomfield valued Hardy's work for him and put his name forward to be a member of the Architectural Association.

Meanwhile, he attended Charles Dickens's public lecture and spent time exploring the scientific and cultural offerings of London society, visiting museums and galleries, and seeing plays and operas. Further reading included the word of Herbert Spencer, Thomas Henry Huxley, John Stuart Mill, John Ruskin and Charles Darwin. The combined effect of these writers was to cause him to abandon plans of ordination in the Anglican Church, becoming increasingly disillusioned with the more institutional forms of Christianity. His own poetry flourished, spurred on by reading Robert Browning and Algernon Charles Swinburne, though it was still rejected for publication. He wrote the satire How I Built Myself a House in 1865, published in Chambers Journal and which was the first of his work to achieve recognition, winning him a prize. He also persevered with his poetry, though it remained unpublished.

By 1867 Hardy had grown tired of London and returned to Bockhampton to resume his work with John Hicks. He embarked on a love affair with his cousin, Tryphena, who lived nearby and, though there is little historical evidence of their relationship, had a profound effect on his writing at the time and appears in various guises throughout the poetry he wrote then, while also in the more obviously dedicated poem 'Thoughts of Phena'. He now began his first novel, The Poor Man and the Lady, which he submitted to Alexander Macmillan, a publishing house. Though Macmillan himself chose not to publish it, he encouraged Hardy to continue writing, and Hardy was advised to concentrate on his plotting. John Hicks's death in 1869 caused Hardy to move to Weymouth seeking employment, and at the same time he began Desperate Remedies, also refused by Macmillan but later published anonymously in three volumes by William Tinsley, in 1871. This publication saw him resolve to dedicate himself fully to his writing, though he was not yet in a position to achieve financial security or literary success. His second published novel, Under the Greenwood Tree, appeared in 1872 and its favourable reception encouraged the publication of A Pair of Blue Eyes in 1873, the most autobiographical of his novels. Next came Far From the Madding Crowd in 1874, bringing with it critical acclaim, the attention of the public and ultimately financial success. 1878 saw more success with The Return of the Native, and the ensuing years saw him rise to ever greater popularity. By now he had developed the fictional Wessex and resolved to set all of his novels there.

It was while he was working on the restoration of a church in St. Juliot, Cornwall, that he met Emma Lavinia Gifford, the local rector's sister-in-law. Captivated by her looks and her admiration for him, he fell in love with her and she would encourage his prose and poetry writing, attracted by his literary capabilities. It took them four years to marry, though, on 17th September 1874 in St Peters Church, Paddington, London. They were both thirty at marriage, though he thought she looked younger and she thought he looked older. None of Hardy's family attended the service. In 1885 the couple settled near Dorchester at Max Gate, a large mid-Victorian villa, designed by Hardy and where he spent the rest of his life. He felt very comfortable there, calling it his country retreat. The Mayor of Casterbridge was published in 1886, and its fictional setting bears many similarities to Dorchester, the market town which he knew so well. He and Emma journeyed to Italy in 1887, returning via Paris and London.

Tess of the d'Urbervilles was published in 1891 to the shock of the prudish Victorian audience who were dismayed by with the cruel presentation of a young girl's seduction and ruination by a rakish aristocrat. It only saw publication after Hardy made extensive alterations to its plot, editing or deleting vast passages. His last novel, Jude the Obscure, suffered the same levels of public outcry when it was published in 1895, and the uproar over these two novels so disturbed him that he returned to poetry, regarded by him and his audience as a purer form of artistic expression. He had not been able to make enough money as a young man to live off his poetry, but now as an adult living off the success of his novels he was able to survive comfortably, and even had a collection of his earlier poems published under the title Wessex Poems, in 1898. Meanwhile, in 1896 Emma had introduced him to the fashionable new pastime of cycling and he bought a high-quality Rover Cobb bicycle, frequently touring the Dorset countryside with his wife. They travelled extensively, to Paris, the Continent and throughout England, along with a visit to Belgium.

Hardy spent the years between 1903 and 1908 writing The Dynasts, and epic poem in blank verse about the Napoleonic Wars, and his literary authority saw him honoured by the University of Aberdeen with an honourary degree in 1905, bringing with it recognition as one of the most outstanding British authors. George V conferred on him the Order of Merit in 1910 and he was awarded the gold medal of the Royal

Society of Literature in 1912. Further to his honourary degree at Aberdeen, Cambridge University named him a Doctor of Letters, his popularity continuing to grow the entire time. WIth this popularity came the dramatisation and performance of various works, and in 1914 the adaptation of The Dynasts was performed at Kingsway Theatre in London. He now proceeded to sell or donate the majority of his manuscripts, either to museums or collectors.

Emma died suddenly on 27th November 1912, and despite having grown increasingly estranged he was greatly affected by her passing, reproaching himself after her burial for not having realised the extent of her illness. He proceeded to write numerous poems expressing nostalgia for their happier times in youth, and after her death he was now taken care of by his niece and a young woman, Florence Dagdale. She was shy and charming with literary aspirations of her own, having published a few books for children, and again her admiration for him led to his infatuation with her. They married on 6th February 1914, though the wedding quickly deteriorated with it became apparent that Hardy preferred "spending much of each day closeted in his study". By now, he was in his seventies, though in spite of his ages he campaigned in favour of British involvement in the First World War. Many great writers visited him at Max Gate, for he left less and less.

In 1924 hew witnessed a stage production of Tess of the d'Urbervilles, a performance so powerful that Hardy promptly became infatuated with the young actress playing Tess. From 1920 to 1927 he worked, in secret, on his autobiography, which was published in two volumes in 1928 and 1930 as the work of Florence Hardy. She made various emendations to the text, having typed the manuscripts, probably reducing the references to Emma and adding anecdotes and referring to letters. His 87th birthday passed, and he seemed increasingly weaker, staying in bed for long periods, until in 1927 he fell gravely ill, dying on the 11th January 1928. Just prior to his death, he asked Florence to read a verse from The Rubaiyat of Omar Khayyam,

Oh, Thou, who Man of baser Earth didst make,
And ev'n with Paradise devise the snake:
For all the Sin wherewith the Face of Man
Is blackened - Man's forgiveness give - and take!

His body was cremated and the ashes interred in Poet's Corner in the South Transept in Westminster Abbey. The official of the two funerals was attended by the then Prime Minister Stanley Baldwin, leader of the Opposition Ramsay MacDonald, the heads of Oxford and Cambridge University colleges where Hardy had been honoured, and various significant literary figures such as James Barrie, George Bernard Shaw and Rudyard Kipling. Meanwhile, his heart was buried alongside his first wife in Stinsford churchyard, Dorchester. He is best remembered by Evelyn Hardy, the critic, who writes "Hardy's life was not primarily one of action. He was by nature a scholar and a writer: it is what goes on in the mind that holds us, and Hardy's was rich with stored impressions".

THOMAS HARDY – A CONCISE BIBLIOGRAPHY

Prose

Hardy divided his novels and collected short stories into three types

Novels of Character and Environment
The Poor Man and the Lady (1867, unpublished and now lost)
Under the Greenwood Tree: A Rural Painting of the Dutch School (1872)
Far from the Madding Crowd (1874)
The Return of the Native (1878)
The Mayor of Casterbridge: The Life and Death of a Man of Character (1886)
The Woodlanders (1887)
Wessex Tales (1888, a collection of short stories)
Tess of the d'Urbervilles: A Pure Woman Faithfully Presented (1891)
Life's Little Ironies (1894, a collection of short stories)
Jude the Obscure (1895)

Romances and Fantasies
A Pair of Blue Eyes: A Novel (1873)
The Trumpet-Major (1880)
Two on a Tower: A Romance (1882)
A Group of Noble Dames (1891, a collection of short stories)
The Well-Beloved: A Sketch of a Temperament (1897) (first published as a serial from 1892)

Novels of Ingenuity
Desperate Remedies: A Novel (1871)
The Hand of Ethelberta: A Comedy in Chapters (1876)
A Laodicean: A Story of To-day (1881)

Short Stories
How I Built Myself A House (1865)
Destiny and a Blue Cloak (1874)
The Thieves Who Couldn't Stop Sneezing (1877)
The Duchess of Hamptonshire (1878)
The Distracted Preacher (1879)
Fellow-Townsmen (1880)
The Honourable Laura (1881)
What The Shepherd Saw (1881)
A Tradition of Eighteen Hundred and Four (1882)
The Three Strangers (1883)
The Romantic Adventures of a Milkmaid (1883)
Interlopers at the Knap (1884)
A Mere Interlude (1885)

A Tryst at an Ancient Earthwork (1885)
Alicia's Diary (1887)
The Waiting Supper (1887–88)
The Withered Arm (1888)
A Tragedy of Two Ambitions (1888)
The First Countess of Wessex (1889)
Anna, Lady Baxby (1890)
The Lady Icenway (1890)
Lady Mottisfont (1890)
The Lady Penelope (1890)
The Marchioness of Stonehenge (1890)
Squire Petrick's Lady (1890)
Barbara of the House of Grebe (1890)
The Melancholy Hussar of The German Legion (1890)
Absent-Mindedness in a Parish Choir (1891)
The Winters and the Palmleys (1891)
For Conscience' Sake (1891)
Incident in Mr. Crookhill's Life (1891)
The Doctor's Legend (1891)
Andrey Satchel and the Parson and Clerk (1891)
The History of the Hardcomes (1891)
Netty Sargent's Copyhold (1891)
On The Western Circuit (1891)
A Few Crusted Characters: Introduction (1891)
The Superstitious Man's Story (1891)
Tony Kytes, the Arch-Deceiver (1891)
To Please His Wife (1891)
The Son's Veto (1891)
Old Andrey's Experience as a Musician (1891)
Our Exploits At West Poley (1892–93)
Master John Horseleigh, Knight (1893)
The Fiddler of the Reels (1893)
An Imaginative Woman (1894)
The Spectre of the Real (1894)
A Committee-Man of 'The Terror' (1896)
The Duke's Reappearance (1896)
The Grave by the Handpost (1897)
A Changed Man (1900)
Enter a Dragoon (1900)
Blue Jimmy: The Horse Stealer (1911)
Old Mrs. Chundle (1929)
The Unconquerable (1992)

Poetry Collections

Wessex Poems and Other Verses (1898)
Poems of the Past and the Present (1901)
Time's Laughingstocks and Other Verses (1909)
Satires of Circumstance (1914)
Moments of Vision (1917)
Collected Poems (1919)
Late Lyrics and Earlier with Many Other Verses (1923)
Human Shows, Far Phantasies, Songs and Trifles (1925)
Winter Words in Various Moods and Metres (1928)

Drama

The Dynasts: An Epic-Drama of the War with Napoleon (verse drama)
The Dynasts, Part 1 (1904)
The Dynasts, Part 2 (1906)
The Dynasts, Part 3 (1908)
The Famous Tragedy of the Queen of Cornwall at Tintagel in Lyonnesse (1923) (one-act play)